Survivin
Toxic Family

Taking yourself out of the equation and taking your life back from your dysfunctional family

Publisher's note:

This book is not intended as a substitute for the advice of a professional mental health counselor. The reader should consult a therapist or counselor in matters relating to his/her emotional and behavioral health and particularly with respect to any symptoms that may require diagnosis or medical attention.

The stories presented in this book are composites. All names and identifying details have been changed to protect the privacy of individuals.

This book is dedicated to my clients. Through you I have been given the opportunity to live so many lives and experience so many different worlds. You have made my life so much richer. You have taught me so much.

Chapters

Introduction

Jennifer never quite felt like she belonged. Growing up, her parents were too busy with their own issues and "concerns" to really give her the attention she needed. There was little parental supervision and because of this her siblings terrorized her. It seemed that her only purpose for being in the family was to serve as "comic relief" or for others to take out their aggression on. Things weren't much better when she was school-aged. The other kids at school picked on her and she was the frequently the tag-line in jokes. Jennifer learned that it was better to just not say anything. So she stopped talking and stopped trying to make friends. She would eat her lunch in the school bathroom in order to avoid these painful social interactions.

As an adult she always worked hard. Objectively, she was the best employee everywhere she ever worked, yet she never received a single "employee of the month" or promotion. Despite her qualifications and years of experience, she was very low on the totem pole. In general, she felt invisible.

She was equally hard-working and giving with her relationships. Yet, the times when she needed other people the most, she frequently found herself rejected, exploited, and abandoned. She just couldn't understand why other people treated her the way they did. It was as if she was cursed. All she knew for certain was that it all began as a child growing up in a dysfunctional family.

Maybe you can't relate exactly to Jennifer's story, but if you are reading this book it's because you believe that you too grew up in a dysfunctional family and are still in the process of trying to recover from that experience. Even as an adult, you see that the experience has affected you. The families we grow up in can set a theme for the rest of our life: a theme where we are mistreated by others, used up and exploited, under-appreciated, rarely respected, and not living up to our potential.

Why did this happen to us? Why does it continue to happen? Because starting at a very young age, you became part of an equation, and despite your best efforts, you keep being put back into that equation time and time again. Here's an example of what some of these equations can look like:

Alcoholic dad + Enabling mom + Angry siblings + You = Dysfunction

Depressed mother+ Abusive step-father + You = Dysfunction

Drug-addicted parent + Foster care system + You = Dysfunction

Narcissistic mother + Pedophile relative + You = Dysfunction

Chronically unemployed and financially irresponsible parents + Abusive siblings + You = Dysfunction

The examples above are by no means exhaustive. They are just a few of the many forms that a dysfunctional family can take. But either way, there was certainly a formula or equation when it came to you and your family. Each person had a specific role in the family, including you. What was your role in the equation? Let's take a look at some of the common roles children of dysfunctional families find themselves in. You may found that your role in your family was a mix of more than one of these or maybe even changed over time:

- **The Giver:** The giver is the person in the family who gives and gives and gives and gets very little back in return. You receive little appreciation from your family despite giving so much. You don't get acknowledgment because it's *expected* that you give; that's just your role in the family. People selfishly use you to fulfill their own needs. This comes to its extreme when a parent or other family member uses the child to fulfill their sexual needs. The child, ever the giver, feels pressure to keep their sexual abuse a secret in order to prevent disrupting the family. As an adult, you may still be supporting your family financially or emotionally. Your family thinks nothing of asking you for rent money or calling you up late at night to vent about their latest crisis. Of course, when you need a similar favor they are nowhere to be found. You've probably noticed a similar pattern with your friends. You give your friendships so much and they are always eager to accept what you offer, but you still find yourself excluded from parties or other social gatherings. At work you take on extra assignments and do the work no one else is willing to do. You know you are a good worker and yet, like Jennifer, you never get that recognition.

- **The Punching Bag:** Your role was to be the one that everyone let their frustrations out on. When your parents were frustrated with their marriage or dealing with work stress, you were the one they took it out on via physical or emotional abuse. Your siblings may have done the same thing. Maybe you were the youngest so as the smaller one it was easier to physically over-power you or come up with clever ways to make fun of you. This role continued in school where you were often bullied. In your relationships you may have also found that you get "dumped on" by your significant others. People use you to let off steam. You may have also gotten the impression from important people in your life that it's not okay for you to have negative feelings, only they can. It's as if your feelings are not a consideration at all.

- **The Scape-Goat:** You just can't do anything right. It's never good enough no matter how much you accomplish or how hard you try. You are perpetually blamed. Even if things have nothing to do with you, somehow it gets twisted so it's your fault. If you put a glass of water on the table and another family member knocks it over, then it's your fault because you had the nerve to put a glass of water on the table. This blaming can go so far that clients have reported telling me that as children they were blamed for their parent's affairs, gambling addictions, missed promotions at work, and social problems. Although it sounds ridiculous to blame an 8 year old for your choice to have an extra-marital affair, after a while the child may come to believe that they deserve this blame. After being blamed so much, the blame gets internalized. What used to be the message of other people becomes the child's own message. As an adult the scapegoat becomes the fall guy at work and with their significant others. The equation continues.

- **The Confidant**: Being the confidant of a toxicl family doesn't seem as bad as the other roles listed here, but it is still damaging and harmful to a child who is put in that role. The confidant is the one who gets put in the role as a sort of therapist to one or both parents. The parent confesses their secrets, complains to the child about the other family members, and in general confides to the child about adult matters. Seemingly nothing is off limits to the parents of the confidant. I have heard of parents telling their child about their extra-marital affairs, traumas, and even suicidal inclinations. The child comes to feel responsible for the parent's emotional well-being. This may even generalize to the point that the child feels responsible for just about everyone's feelings. This act of using your child as a confidant has been given the provocative (and controversial) term of "emotional incest" to demonstrate just how damaging it is for the child to be put in that role. My adult clients who were confidants as children often report taking other people's emotions very personally. They feel responsible when other people are upset. Even as adults it's not unusual for family to try to keep them in this role.
- **The Invisible One**: The invisible one is just that, invisible. As a child you learned that the best way to survive in your

dysfunctional family was to just lie low. You never made any "noise" or demands. You never asked for anything. You knew not to expect anything. Perhaps you even received praise from your parents for being this way, i.e. "Sara never asks for anything!" Your siblings most likely took advantage of you and you complained about it as little as possible. As a child you were very responsible. You learned to "self-parent". You did your homework without needing to be reminded or supervised. You got a job as soon as you were old enough to. You were the child no one had to worry about. But even still, you had very few friends and would be described as an extreme introvert. You like being alone and only having to worry about yourself. As an adult, your independence and self-sufficiency most likely paid-off when you compare yourself to your siblings, and yet you find you receive no praise from your parents. You are invisible still. One of my clients relayed to me "I could become the first female President of the United States and my family still wouldn't be impressed. I've accomplished more than anyone else in the family but they act as though they don't notice. When I point out these things, I just get a blank stare and then they change the subject to my sister." As an adult the invisible one often suffers from depression.

- **The Caregiver:** The Caregiver is the one who takes care of everyone. When things get tough, people call you to try to fix it. Even as a child your needs came dead last. Perhaps you acted as a sort of stand-in parent while your parents were away at work. Even as a child, it may have fallen to you to help pay the bills. It is not unusual for the caregiver to get a job as soon as they are legally old enough to and to balance school and a nearly full-time job. The caregiver is held to a double standard. They are expected to keep it together but no one else in the family is. They are the responsible one while everyone else gets a free pass. This need-based relationship continues into adulthood where the caregiver is the perpetual "fixer" in the family. The caregiver is responsible not just for paying their bills but perhaps even those of their adult siblings. Of course, it is expected that the caregiver is the one who will take in their parents when they become elderly. If the caregiver ever complains, the family becomes angry or irritated with them. The caregiver feels very much depleted and under appreciated by those around them. Worse yet, they know that most of the people in their family are too selfish or incapable to help them if they ever needed it.

- **The Manipulator:** The manipulator is just that, a child who manipulates and takes advantage of the dysfunctional nature of the family. Let's use an example: Dad has a gambling addiction. Due to this, Mom hides money from Dad so she'll have money to pay the bills. Sometimes dad finds the hidden money and spends it on lottery tickets. This addiction and the money it takes to fuel it has caused many hardships for the family. Rather than go without like the other children, the manipulator always has cash in his pocket. He finds where Mom hides the money and skims some money off the top. If Mom notices money is missing from her stash, she blames Dad. Thus the manipulator is able to get ahead in a family where few are able to. Another classic manipulator move is to turn family members against each other. In this way they are able to "divide & conquer". Their goal is to slowly gain control and influence. There is often an odd love/hate relationship between parents and the manipulator. The parents resent their inability to control the manipulator, often feel the manipulator is a disappointment, yet give more to the manipulator than they do to the other children. As an adult, the manipulator continues to con their family members out of money, favors, and even their inheritance.

- **The "Good" One:** When you grow up in a chaotic family where everyone has issues, naturally some children decide that there isn't enough room in the family for there to be yet another person with something wrong with them. The family needs someone to be the "good one", and since all the other roles have been taken, the child strives to be extra good in order to try to lift up the rest of the family. The child thinks "Maybe if I'm really good, it'll tip the scales enough for this to be a sort of normal family." Although the child just wants to be good and add some positivity to the family, it is not unusual for them to be resented by their siblings. As the child gets older, they become very much concerned with the family legacy. They may choose a high-prestige career path or in some other way try to make the family proud. It's a lot of pressure for a young adult. When you become adults they are people pleasers. They try to fit whatever role they think will be pleasing to others. They may not even have a clear idea of who they really are as a person or what they really want out of life.

- **The "Bad" One:** When a child grows up in a household that can best be described as "dysfunctional" it is not at all unusual for them to respond in kind. Often times you find that so-called "problem children" were fine in their early years; it wasn't until they start interacting with other children and those children's families that they realize that theirs is not normal. They start to question that maybe it's not okay that Mom rages after she's come home from work and had a few. Maybe it's not okay that late at night my step-dad comes into their bedroom and touches them while they pretend to sleep. Maybe other kid's parents don't fight all the time. Once the child realizes that things are not okay at home, they sort of "sound the alarm" with disruptive behavior. Their behavior screams "What's going on here is not okay! I'm not okay! Why can't you see that this family isn't normal?!" But the family doesn't get the message. They think that the child is just bad. It's not unusual for the family to send the child to therapy or some other program. Back when I worked predominantly as a child therapist I would see children like this all the time. When I pointed out to the parent that it wasn't that the child was bad or mentally ill, but that the parent just needed to make some changes in the family, the parent would fire me as the therapist. The family doesn't want to change. They want the child to conform or fall into line; to be "okay" with the dysfunction like the other kids in the family. Another reason for the child's "bad behavior" may have been because they were crying out for someone to pay attention to them. In dysfunctional families it is not unusual for the parent to be so self-centered or so distracted with their own "stuff" that the child is crying out for some kind of acknowledgment. For some kids, the only time they could get any kind of emotion from their parent was when the parent became furious towards them. This anger, although certainly not ideal, was at least a sign that the parent cared enough to become angry with them. One client reported to me that he would purposefully push his mother's buttons to the point that she would slap him across the face. It made him feel important or special that he could cause her to get so angry with him. He told me "I begged for that slap." These children often leave the home at a young age, pretty much as soon as they are old enough to. They may do this by joining the military, going to college out of state, or becoming pregnant and moving in with a boyfriend. Once out of the home, they often do fairly well for themselves.

Did any of these roles sound familiar to you? Perhaps you found that you had more than one role, such as being the "good one" and "the confidant". Or perhaps you found that your role changed as you got older or after someone else left the family. You may also recognize your siblings or other family members in the descriptions of these roles. As I mentioned in each description, these roles given to us in childhood often follow us in adulthood. However, that is not always the case. Some people rebel against the roles given to them when they reach young adulthood. The person puts their foot down and refuses to ever be a caregiver or punching bag to someone else ever again. Although this may seem to be a step in the right direction, the person will sometimes take things to such an extreme as to be just as damaging as the original role.

Why I wrote this book

And this is why I wrote this book. I see so many clients that have suffered and continue to suffer because of their dysfunctional families. They often grow up feeling very confused by other people. They don't understand why they get rejected socially or are perpetually exploited and taken advantage of by other people. It is a never ending pattern and it seems like no matter what they do the pattern never changes. They feel that they are cursed or destined to suffer in life. They just cannot understand why this keeps happening to them despite always trying to do the "right thing" and being nice to other people.

They ask themselves "Is it me? I don't think I do things to deserve this treatment from other people, but maybe I do? Maybe there's just something about me that rubs people the wrong way. I don't know what it is exactly, but there must be something really bad about me that other people don't like." So they decide that they must somehow deserve this abuse and obviously that's a very depressing thought. Once someone makes this decision about themselves, it will sabotage their entire life.

The truth is it's not your fault. At a very young age you were put into an environment where you had to fit a certain role in order to survive. In order to make it in this family, you had to fit into the equation. You may have even had experiences growing up where you saw how people who refused to fit into the dysfunctional equation were rejected or cut off from the family. As a child who doesn't have any other options, the risk of that happening was too great, so you found your way into the equation.

As adults, we are attracted to what is familiar to us. The dysfunctional equation is all we have known growing up and we unconsciously put ourselves back into the equation time and time again. Let's say you had a cruel older brother growing up. You may find that you tend to date men very much like your brother. Perhaps you work places where the boss or supervisor is also cruel. This isn't to say you meet a guy and think "Wow, this guy's such a jerk. I think I'll date him!" No one's saying that. Obviously there is something good that initially pulls you in and by the time you consciously realize that the guy is a jerk it's too late.

I see this all the time with my clients and think it is so sad that they were able to survive their childhood only to be forced to continuously relive it in adulthood. It is especially sad to see them take the mistreatment so personally. They are all such good people who deserve to be appreciated and loved for who they are, not for what they can provide for people who don't even appreciate it. Lastly it makes me sad because I know that it doesn't have to be this way.

As you will learn through reading this book, the effects of growing up in a dysfunctional family do not have to be a life sentence. There is a recovery. There is a normal life out there for you. You can take control. Time and time again I've seen my clients be able to take their life back.

I would love to take on as a client everyone who has struggled with this issue and personally guide them through recovery, but as I've learned I have my limits. One limit is time. I can only see so many clients in a day. There simply are not enough hours in the day to see all of the clients who want my help. Another limit is location. I am here in Boston, MA. Sure, many of my clients have traveled out of State to see me, but there are still limits to how far people can go in order to come to my office. By writing a book, my ability to reach and help others is almost limitless.

Another limit is that I know that there are a lot of people out there who are struggling with this issue but are simply unwilling to see a therapist at this time. Perhaps this is due to fear, shame, or other limiting beliefs and negative feelings about seeing a therapist. For them, this book can be a step in the right direction.

What is a dysfunctional family?

Before we go any further, I should address what a dysfunctional family is exactly. A lot of people question if their family is truly dysfunctional or if every family has some amount of dysfunction in it and so should be considered normal. I've noticed a recent trend in the media and popular belief where the term "dysfunctional family" has come to mean "quirky, unconventional, off-beat, fun, casual". That is certainly not the definition I am using and is not the definition used by mental health professionals.

Mental health professionals such as myself define a dysfunctional family as a family where individuals are not able to thrive physically and/or emotionally. If you were to think about the "function" of a family, the basic function is for parents to be able to provide a healthy and nurturing environment for their children. This environment thus allows the children to grow up to be emotionally mature individuals who know how to function well in society and live up to their full potential as individuals.

When a family is dysfunctional, the result is the opposite of that: The children are not physically healthy, either because they are neglected or abused physically or sexually. The children develop emotional scars due to interacting with parents or other family members who are not emotionally healthy. They have difficulty getting along socially because their social-model at home was mostly one of continuous conflict. Rather than grow up to reach their full potential as adults, they are instead "handicapped" by the experience.

I'm always amazed by the number of clients I have who never realized before that their family was dysfunctional. To them it was just normal. Domestic violence in the household was excused away as "but everybody's parents fought." An older cousin who molested them was "just experimenting with his sexuality. We were both kids. Kids do that kind of thing." And yet, as much as they don't want to face the horrible experiences they had as a child, they still have the emotional and behavioral consequences of someone who grew up in a toxic family.

You may be asking yourself right now "Did I really have a dysfunctional family? Some dysfunction is still normal, right?" It's true that there is no such thing as a perfect family. I'm yet to meet one, and believe me, I'm always on the lookout. No parent is perfect. Our parents are people with flaws just like us. I truly believe that most parents are doing the best they can for their children even when they're not doing a perfect job at it. Parenting is hard and children have a lot of needs. Parents also have their own needs and it's impossible for a parent to fulfill all of their own needs and their children's needs. At some point someone's needs will go unfulfilled, and I'm not saying that parents should necessarily sacrifice their own needs all the time.

I think that in most dysfunctional families, the parents really were trying to do the best they could for their family, they just had too much of their own "stuff" to be effective parents. It is possible to be in a dysfunctional family where your parents loved you and cared about you. Accepting that you were in a dysfunctional family doesn't mean you have to hate your parents or believe that they never loved you. It simply means accepting the reality of the situation and putting in the effort to understand what happened to you as a child so that you do not have to keep repeating the pattern of dysfunction.

If you're still questioning whether you grew up in a toxic or dysfunctional family, one way therapists determine this is by the level of distress experienced by the client. Growing up, was home a stressful environment? Did you fantasize about running away from home? Did you actually run away from home? Did you turn to drugs or alcohol to try to alleviate the negative feelings caused by your family? Even as an adult, does spending time with your family cause you distress? Do you feel dread leading up to family get-togethers?

The way you feel about your family is a big indicator of whether the family was dysfunctional or not. Looking back, do you feel that if you had grown up in a functional family that you would be better off today emotionally, physically, and socially? Does the family *feel* toxic to you? If you believe that you have a dysfunctional family, the odds are likely that you probably do. Of course, it's not at all an uncommon reaction for a dysfunctional family to say "It's not us! You're the one who's sick!" After hearing this over and over again throughout your life, this may be why you're having doubts now. On some level, you feel that perhaps you are the toxic one.

Maybe you're starting to accept that your family is dysfunctional, but you don't think the dysfunction was as severe as the stories in this book or other families you know off. Just because there is worst dysfunction out there doesn't mean that what you went through doesn't hurt, wasn't significant, or wasn't important. Nearly every client I've had that has a dysfunctional family could think of another family that had it worse than them. That doesn't mean that their suffering doesn't count. That doesn't mean that they should just "count their blessings" because there are people out there who have it worse than them.

It doesn't matter that there are people out there who have it worse than you do. If your family causes you distress or discomfort or has prevented you from living up to your potential, then you can do something about it. The suffering caused to you by your family is unnecessary. There is no reason why you have to be tortured. If you don't like the way they treat you, you don't have to put up with that any longer. In addition to dealing with the immediate effects of being in a dysfunctional family, you can also do something about the lasting effects of having been in a dysfunctional family.

The lasting effects of being in a toxic family

Even if you manage to "escape" from your dysfunctional family in adulthood, the experience of having been in a dysfunctional family can have lasting effects. For me, this is one of the saddest things about having grown up in a dysfunctional family: even if you leave, the dysfunction tends to follow you. What are some of those lasting effects? I'm going to describe them here. Of course, these symptoms alone do not mean that a person is from a dysfunctional family and lack of symptoms does not mean that what you experienced in childhood was insignificant:

- **Low self-confidence:** People from dysfunctional families often repeatedly get the message that they are not good enough. No matter what they do for the family, it's never enough. After being told this again and again, they lose their sense of confidence. Once you lose your confidence, it can be very hard to gain it back. It tends to be a downward spiral for many people. If you really think about it, it's very hard to succeed when you lack confidence. You second guess yourself, you hesitate, and because of that, you mess up. For a lot of people, it starts out as a lack of confidence at home because they feel they can never please their parent. Then they start doubting themselves at school and they come to believe that they no longer have the ability to do well academically. Their lack of confidence causes them to do poorly in sports as well. They get poor grades or always get picked last in gym class. This kills their self-confidence even more. Some children from dysfunctional families will actually excel academically or in sports, but suffer from a lack of confidence when it comes to social interactions. Even as an adult this low self-confidence can continue to plague you and sabotage your efforts.

- **Under-recognition:** People from dysfunctional households are often very good at school and are hard workers. I wonder if this is because they see from an early age that they really can only depend on themselves so they strive to work hard and be extra good in school or sports in order to provide themselves with an "out" when they're old enough to leave. Perhaps they are still holding on to the hope that they could make their parents proud of them, but just like how they don't receive the recognition they crave from their parents, they tend to not receive that recognition from their teachers nor from their employers later on in life. Sure, people may say "You're a hard worker" or "You're a good student", but those efforts never seem to pay off in the form of real recognition such as a promotion or a leadership role. Their careers are stagnant and they can never seem to get ahead despite having great potential and working so hard.

- **Low Self-esteem:** In general, people from dysfunctional families don't feel good about themselves. They look back on the way that they were treated, continue to be treated, and wonder if they deserve it. When a person has low self-esteem, they feel that they have low worth as a person. They feel that other people are more worthy than they are. The truth is no one's better than anyone else. You are not less worthy than other people. Each of us has a special purpose in life. My life path is to provide guidance and nurturing to others. What's your life path? You'll find that when you live a life true to your path, problems with self-esteem start to go away. We'll talk about this more in the last two chapters of the book, but first it's important that you have a better grasp on why your family acts the way they do.

- **Irritability / Angry Outbursts:** This may be a habit you picked up in childhood when you were trying to communi-cate to your family that everything was not okay. However, there are other possibilities. Anger is something that is rarely understood in our society. When people see an angry person they think "That guy's a jerk" or "She's just a bad person". They don't understand that anger comes from a place of hurt. Both anger and sadness come from the same place; they're just different reactions. When an adult has problems with anger or irritability, especially in their relationships, it's often because their needs are not being met. They feel depleted, and this depletion makes them prone to being easily frustrated and irritated by the behaviors of others. It's not so easy to just "let it go" when you're running on empty. My angry clients find that things stop bothering them once they start prioritizing their needs.

It's easy to see how this can happen. When you grow up in a dysfunctional family, you're taught that your needs aren't important or that your needs come last. It's then natural for such a person to never learn things like self-care. Once they do, anger issues become less of a probkem.

- **Alcohol abuse & Addiction:** Drug use and other addictive behaviors are not at all uncommon in dysfunctional families. Growing up, the odds are likely that you had a parent or sibling that was abusing drugs or alcohol. There may have also been other addictions like gambling or over-indulgence in food. Life can feel very chaotic and hopeless in a toxic family. It's natural to want to escape that. Some choose to escape it through drugs or alcohol. You may have found in your teen or pre-teen years that alcohol or drugs were a way to cope with those negative feelings. A lot of people have told me that things were so chaotic and tense at home that the only way they could fall asleep at night was by drinking or smoking marijuana in the evenings. This habit may have followed you into adulthood. There are better ways of relaxing and "turning your brain off". If you have a problem, or suspect you have a problem with drugs, alcohol, or other addictive behaviors, then you really should see a pro-fessional.
- **Being a Loner:** A "loner" is someone who prefers being alone. They may only have one or two friends. When they do have friends, they are very selective over who is their friend and will easily "drop" a friendship at the first sign that the person is not trustworthy or does not respect them. They will also often choose to get the majority of their socialization from their significant other. Loners are very sensitive to social rejection and may have experienced a lot of it early on in life, such as first or second grade. As someone from a dysfunctional family, you learned from an early age that you can't trust people. It is also very likely that your parents never taught you proper social skills and this led you to be rejected socially at an early age. After

having such bad experiences, you may have decided that it's better to just be alone.

- **Over-scheduled:** This is sort of the opposite of the loner. You may have learned early on that having a lot of friends and an active social life was a way to get away from your dysfunctional family. You used friends and after-school activities as a way to be home as little as possible. Even after you moved out of your parent's house, this habit may have followed you. In general, people would describe you as being over-scheduled. You have many social obligations and hobbies that keep you busy. Part of you likes keeping busy but part of you wishes you could have more time to breathe. You may even find yourself feeling resentful about being pulled in so many directions by friends and family.

- **People Pleaser:** Would you describe yourself as being a "people pleaser"? People pleasers want to be liked by other people. Pleasing and satisfying other people is very important to them, perhaps even more important than pleasing themselves. They give so much to their jobs, significant others, and families. Other people's happiness always comes first. And yet, the people pleaser feels that they repeatedly fail at their task. Despite all of the effort they put into it, they are always in fear that others don't like them or are unhappy with them. Due to this, they have a strong tendency to be exploited by other people. People take advantage of their giving nature and try to take as much as they can get. In the office they are over-worked. At home they may find themselves as both the bread-winner and the one responsible for the majority of the house work. It's not unusual to find that they marry a partner who suffers from a vague (others may suspect that the person is just "making it up" or "milking it") medical condition that prevents them from working full time or helping out in the home.

- **Zero Tolerance:** The opposite of the people pleaser is the person who has zero tolerance for the wants or needs of other people. You learned in childhood that you couldn't please your family no matter how hard you tried so you gave up. In fact, you gave up on trying to please anyone. The only person you can make happy is yourself, so you focus on that. And if other people don't like your attitude? Well, no one's forcing them to hang out with you. You find you have zero interest or patience for trying to please other people. If they can't take you as you are, oh well. Other people have complained to you about your "tone" or "the way" you say things, but you don't see what the problem is with the tone of voice you use. That's just the way you talk. Other people have accused you of being abrasive, off-putting, or too intense. You secretly feel hurt by the rejection but feel powerless to change things. You may even feel like its other people who need to change. You wonder why people won't put in more of an effort when they are in a relationship with you.

- **History of Bad Relationships:** You have a pattern of bad relationships. Friends may complain that you have a pattern of dating bad people. What do I mean by "bad"? You tend to date people that you end up taking care of financially and/or emotionally. You do the majority of the work or effort in the relationship. The other person "strings you along" by repeatedly breaking up with you and then getting back together. Like your family of origin, the relationship would not be described as stable. Any disagreement or argument ends in threats of ending the relationship. The people you date don't respect you and they demonstrate this by cheating on you, criticizing or insulting you, not keeping you in the loop, and being chronically unreliable. You don't know how this keeps happening to you. When you first meet them they seem so nice, then they change once they get settled into the relationship. You're starting to wonder if there are such things as "good men" or "good women" out there. Or maybe it's just you? You wonder if maybe there's something about you that causes good people to go bad. There isn't, but naturally you would think this after so many bad experiences.

As I mentioned before, you don't need to have all of these in order to be from a dysfunctional family. In fact, some of the things I listed are contradictory, so you wouldn't be able to exhibit all of these at once. However, probably several of these rang true for you and you may have even felt like I was reading your mind. As awful as the lasting effects of having grown up in a dysfunctional family are, it's important to realize that these do not have to be a life sentence. You don't have to suffer with these symptoms any longer. I can show you how to end the cycle.

Consider seeing a therapist

I have given this book my all, however, there is only so much a book can do. A book, no matter how well written, cannot replace a therapist or counselor. A book cannot listen to you while you tell your story of abuse and neglect. A book cannot answer your questions or provide you with feedback. A book cannot show you empathy or compassion. A book cannot be there for you when you need support. A book cannot give you an individually-tailored plan for moving your life forward. Those are all things I am able to do for my clients as their therapist but cannot do for you as the author of the book that you are reading now.

Does that mean that this book is useless? Absolutely not! You will still find this book to be an invaluable resource, one that gets you started on the right path. This book is going to provide you with detailed instructions for taking your life back from your dysfunctional family. Of course, we've all had that experience where we read a self-help book, loved the book and believed in its message, but just couldn't follow through when it came time to put the book into practice. Does that mean we are lazy or hopeless? No! It just means that we need the guidance of a therapist to put things in motion, and no should feel bad about that if that is the case for them.

As a therapist, I know that self-help is very beneficial. For some people it's the answer. A good book can change your life. I hope that for you this is that book. However I also know that for other people, self-help is just the first step. For those people, a book like this one provides the person with understanding, insight, and hope. For them, this book will give them strength and give them the knowledge that their life could be better. That will be what they need to finally have the courage to see a therapist.

This book can serve as an excellent way to enhance therapy also. You can talk with your therapist about the things you read in this book or use it as a way to "extend" the therapy session by reading the book in-between appointments. If you've never seen a therapist before, this book can give you an idea of what therapy is like and the kinds of advice that therapists give.

Conclusion

This book has three basic goals: The first goal is to give you insight and understanding about your dysfunctional family and how growing up in such an environment has influenced the person you have become. With this insight you can then free yourself from the self-loathing, self-criticism, and self-blame that so often plagues the adult children of dysfunctional families. The second goal is for you to take yourself out of that dysfunctional equation. This goal is especially for those that still have contact with their family and are unhappy with the way the family continues to treat them. I will teach you things you can do to ensure that you are no longer mistreated by them. The final goal of this book is to show you how to become the person you would have been if not for your dysfunctional family. In this sense, you take your life back from your toxic family. In doing so, you also can learn to free yourself from the "lasting effects" I told you about earlier and start to live a happier and more authentic life.

My recommendation is to not skip any chapters. Each chapter and the goal it seeks to accomplish builds a foundation for which you can accomplish the next goal. If you rush through it or skip ahead, you'll find that you'll then be missing that foundation and won't be able to accomplish the other goals described later. I think this book works best when you take your time and allow yourself to think about or linger on any topics that really resonate with you. Take the time to really think about the questions posed in this book. You'll find that the book works better when you take your time rather than just reading through it all in one sitting.

Most importantly, I want you to be patient with yourself during this process. Change is very hard, especially if it's a dysfunctional pattern that your family has been reinforcing for decades. Slip-ups are to be expected and are okay. Just start over and try again. It doesn't mean you're a failure, it just means that you need some practice because this is something that's very new to you.

Part 1

Lifting the Fog

1

Where do dysfunctional families come from?

Joe never knew his father. He was the oldest of four children and to his understanding none of them had the same father. Once a man at the corner store told him he was his father. Although the man had a warm friendly smile, he was missing some teeth and was just not what Joe had imagined his father would look like. He always imagined his father as being well-dressed and more charismatic. This man was none of those things. Joe felt awkward about the encounter and so just shrugged his shoulders and left. He was only eight years old. He didn't know what to make of the experience. When he was older he asked his mother about the man and she told him that he had died a year or two ago. Oh well.

Hi mother always had a different boyfriend living with them. When one would leave it wasn't long until a new one moved in. At the time he couldn't understand why she would do this as she never got along with any of them. Now he knows that she was probably just using them to pay the bills. Sometimes they would have to move out suddenly either to escape an abusive boyfriend or because the landlord was evicting them. It was not uncommon to come home and find he couldn't do his homework because the electricity had been shut off.

As he got older he fantasized about running away from home and starting a new life for himself; a life where his hard work would pay off for him in the form of a stable apartment and decent clothes. Even as a kid he felt that he could do a better job of *handling adult responsibilities than his mother or her boyfriends. He got his opportunity when he was 16. His mother's boyfriend started beating on his younger brother. Joe pulled the man off his brother but in the process received his own beating. So fed up, Joe told his mother that she needed to make a choice: it's either he leaves or the boyfriend leaves. His mother chose her boyfriend over her own son. Joe filled up his backpack with what little he could and headed out on foot immediately.*

Joe never went back to school. He kept working at his after school job but would take as many hours as he could. He found it wasn't that hard to get his own apartment so long as he came in as somebody's roommate and lied about his age. Joe worked hard and eventually learned a trade.

Despite being a driven and hardworking person, he always found himself working paycheck to paycheck. Although he had now been on his own for 20 years, he didn't feel like his life had improved much since when he was a teenager. He just never could get ahead. He got into relationships with women very much like his mother: chronically unemployed, dependent, needy, critical, and verbally abusive. His latest girlfriend had a habit of draining his bank account. It wasn't until the lights got turned off at his apartment that he realized that despite his best efforts, he had repeated the same dysfunction he had witnessed in his childhood. How could he let this happen?

Joe started to think about his mother. He had only spoken to her off and on the past several years. He decided he needed to talk to her. He just had to know where things went wrong in his family. Where had this dysfunction come from?

I have found that for the adult children of dysfunctional families, the question that continues to plague them most is "why?" *Why was my family like this? Why does my family member hate me so much? Why would my brother treat me like this? Why did my father leave us? Why wouldn't mom go see a therapist? Why did my parents have children in the first place?* I have found when working with clients from dysfunctional families that they simply cannot move forward until they have answers to these questions.

The adult children of dysfunctional families are looking for closure. Very few will ever get that closure from their family or from a specific family member. If you have tried talking to them about what happened and weren't able to get anywhere with it, you are not alone. Most people find that when they try to talk to their family about the things that happened in their childhood that the family member either flat-out denies it ever happened, minimizes what happened ("I can't believe you're still talking about that. It really wasn't that big of a deal"), or becomes angry and defensive.

I have even had a number of clients tell me about visiting their parent on their death bed. You would think that on a person's death bed they could put all vanity aside and just be honest with their adult child. After all, it's their last chance to speak to each other, so why not make amends and give a final "gift" to your child? Even in their final hour they couldn't just be kind to their son or daughter. I have heard numerous stories of the soon-to-be-deceased ordering the person out of the hospital room and then requesting that they even be banned from attending their funeral! All because the adult child wanted one last chance to make peace.

Of course, it is not just dysfunctional parents who cannot admit fault; this also extends to other dysfunctional family members. In fact, I would say that it is a hallmark of toxic and dysfunctional people to not be able to admit to their faults or talk about mistakes that have happened in the past. As a rule, they don't talk about things. They instead choose to lie low until they feel that enough time has passed for things to "blow over" and then act like nothing ever happened.

Towards the beginning of my career, when I would have an individual client tell me about their dysfunctional family, the solution seemed clear: we just need to talk it out with the family member. The client had so many questions that seemingly only that person could answer and not knowing the answers were obviously creating a lot of distress for my client. I naïvely encouraged the client to bring their family member to therapy with them next time. When they did, it was a disaster. The family member would deny *absolutely everything*. They would claim to have been perfect and it was in fact my client who was the bad one. They would then go on to try to assassinate my client's character. It was pure cruelty and I deeply regretted putting my client through that.

This is why I no longer offer family therapy as one of my services. If you do decide that it would be helpful to try to confront the dysfunctional family member with the help of a therapist, make sure that you hire a therapist that only does family therapy and is very experienced working with dysfunctional families.

I'm not saying that it's impossible to have an honest conversation with your dysfunctional family member that leads to closure and understanding, just that I see it happen very rarely. If you are reading this book, the odds are likely that you have tried talking to them and making amends but were unsuccessful at it. If it's been a while since the last time you talked to them though it may be worth it to try again now. Some dysfunctional people "mellow out" with age. Not all, but some. You may find them more receptive to what you have to say. You may also find that you too have "mellowed out" with age and will be better able to have a mature and controlled conversation with your family member.

But what if you've tried talking to your family member and don't get anywhere with it? What if it just makes you feel worse afterwards? Part of getting closure may be accepting that this person will never be able to give you closure. As much as it would mean to you to have them put your hand in their hand and say "You weren't the bad one, I was", that will most likely never happen. The person probably also lacks the insight or self-awareness to provide you with real answers as to why they treated you the way they did. Even if they could stop lying about what happened, they probably lack the ability to explain or articulate what you need to hear.

This is something that's very important for you to understand: *There is no logic to the way a dysfunctional person behaves.* You keep trying to understand why they did what they did using a logical mind and this is why you can never make sense of it, because it literally doesn't make any sense. A logical functioning person would not have made the decisions that they made. A logical functioning person would have been happy to have had you in their family and would have treated you better. If you try to use logic to understand or interpret your family's behaviors, you will never understand why they acted the way they do. And given that they think very differently from you do, this is probably why they seemed so confused about your reactions too.

The origins of dysfunctional families

Since the odds are very likely that you will never be able to get a sincere apology or explanation from your family, I will attempt to give you closure through an understanding of dysfunctional families. The first thing you need to understand is that dysfunctional families begin and end with dysfunctional parent/s. It is my belief that dysfunctional families ultimately begin with the decision to create a family. Somewhere along the way there were two people who decided to get together and start a family for the wrong reason.

This is highly controversial, but I do believe that there are wrong reasons for having a family and I've listed some of these reasons below. What makes them controversial is that this line of thinking is very common and there may in fact be readers who also share these beliefs about having children. Due to this, I've included a number of scientific studies demonstrating that these reasons are faulty. I have included these studies not to discourage people from having children, but rather to discourage them from having children for the wrong reasons:

1. **To secure my relationship:** Having a baby does not secure your relationship. And as every single parent knows, having a baby does not *force* someone to be with you. Research has shown that children have a destabilizing effect on

relationships and increase the likelihood that a couple will divorce (Amato, 2010). In fact, childless couples consistently report feeling happier in their marriages and better able to handle conflicts (White, Booth, & Edwards, 1986; DeOllos & Kapinus, 2002;). When the relationship then fails after the child is born, the parent may harbor overt or covert anger and resentment against the child. This anger and resentment could lead to the parent abusing the child later on.

2. **To make me happy:** I feel we do society a great disservice by lying about the realities of having children. The message that society consistently gives us is that children are nothing but pure joy and if you feel otherwise it is because you are a monster. And yet, those of us just casually observing parents can easily see that they are not in a constate state of pure bliss. Could we be wrong in our observations? When our childed friends confess to us that they regret having children is it because they are monsters or mentally ill? Or perhaps it's because having kids isn't all it's cracked up to be? What does the research tell us about the effect having a child has on our happiness? The research consistently shows that having children does not increase happiness. In fact, most of the time it lowers it (Umberson, Pudrovska, & Reczek, 2010). Anyone who has a child hoping that the child will make them happy is going to be disappointed. Many of my clients who come from dys-functional families have told me that they feel that their parents would have been happier if they had never had children.

3. **To feel accomplished:** There are some people who feel for whatever reason that they cannot achieve their own accomplishments. They feel that they slacked off too much, were robbed of opportunities early on in life, or made too many mistakes to have a "successful" life. So they have a child so that their child can do the things they were unable to accomplish. They then get to enjoy their children's

successes by proxy. The parent takes credit for the child's accomplishments. The child's failures are of course their own and subject to great criticism by the parent. In this case, the parent has a child in order to feel that they have accomplished something. The child then has the burden of being responsible for the parent's own lack of accomplishment.

4. **Because I'm afraid of being alone:** Some people see bringing a child into this world as a way of always having someone in their life. Perhaps at an early age they had a series of experiences with abandonment. They see having children as a way of at least having someone in your life who won't abandon you, because children *need* their parents. As the child gets older and seeks more independence, the parent becomes angry. The parent may guilt the child into living in the family home long after they were old enough to move out. The parent may also be hostile towards the adult child's significant other. Generally speaking, they will express negativity towards anything or anyone that they feel is taking their child away from them.

5. **For the family legacy:** The child is born with a purpose, and that purpose is to carry on the family name or in some other way improve the family legacy. In this sense, the child is viewed as property. They are born with a mission and that mission is what you have chosen for them. This puts a great deal of pressure on the child to live up to familial expectations. The child is born due to the parent's own sense of narcissism or vanity.

6. **In order to exit the workforce**: You might be surprised how common this one is. In this scenario you have a woman that is very unsatisfied with her career. I think that it is a very common experience that when first entering the workforce we find that things are not what we expected. The pay is low and the work is grueling when you are entry-level. We feel dissatisfied and disillusioned and wonder if we chose the wrong career. However, those of us who soldier

through these feelings find that after a few years we get good at our careers, climb the career ladder, and the work becomes much more satisfying. However, some women feel unable or unwilling to soldier through. Rather than admit defeat in their careers, they decide that it is more socially acceptable to exit the workforce by becoming a stay at home mom. So they have a child and when that child is school age they have another child, and repeat this process for as long as they can. After the child is born they realize how stressful caring for a child is. They regret abandoning their career but don't know how to dig themselves out of the hole they now find themselves in.

7. **To have someone take care of me:** This could refer to when you are old and infirm or just in your current day-to-day life. There are certainly children who became caretakers to their parent/s at an early age. Some parents have chronic medical conditions and need a home care companion sooner in life. Other adults worry about their retirement. Perhaps they have made bad decisions financially and feel that they cannot recover from them, so they have a child and hope that they can depend on their adult child financially when they are no longer able to work. I recognize that culturally and historically, people have relied on their children to take care of them in old age, but this is simply something that one can no longer rely on. Only 4.2% of elderly adults move in with their adult children. According to the U.S. Bureau of the Census, slightly over 5 percent of the 65+ population occupy nursing homes, congregate care, assisted living, and board-and-care homes. What that means is that 90% of elderly adults are able to take care of themselves or are cared for by their spouse, not their adult children. So not only is relying on your adult children a gamble that rarely ever pays off, it is also a very selfish reason to have children. Instead of allowing your children to make their own decisions and live their own lives, they now have to take care of you.

8. **Because it's just what you do:** Throughout much of history, having children was not a choice. There are still many people in the world for which it is not a choice whether or not you will have children. However, for most people in the Western world it is a choice. We have contraceptive for both men and women and the options for preventing pregnancy and childbirth seem to increase with each passing year. However, despite all of these advances, there are still people who do not understand that having a child is a choice. For them, it's just something that we all do. It's a part of life: you graduate from school, get married, and then start having children. They never really gave it much thought, but if they had, there's a strong possibility that they would have decided not to. They find later that they don't enjoy parenting, aren't in a financial situation to support their family, and don't have the coping skills to deal with the stress and lack of sleep of having children.

9. **To make my parents happy:** There are people who only have children because they want to give their parents grandchildren. Perhaps they are people pleasers or have always struggled to make their parents proud of them. They may decide that giving their parents adorable grandchildren is the way to finally make them happy, only to find that the grandparents are as indifferent to the grandchildren as they were to them growing up.

10. **No reason:** This is probably the most common reason why people have children: There was no reason. Birth controlled failed, the person wanted to get pregnant someday but not now or by this person, or they were simply shocked one day to discover that they were pregnant. According to the CDC, 40% of births in the United States were unintended. The parents did not plan to get pregnant and did not wish to have the child, and yet they did. Due to this, one could argue that they did not have a child for any reason. The children born under these circumstances are much more likely to live in poverty, have behavioral and emotional

problems, as well as grow up to hold low-paying jobs or have criminal records.

Having children for any of the reasons above doesn't doom someone to being a dysfunctional parent or having a dysfunctional family. There are a lot of people who have children for one of the above reasons and they are able to adjust to become normal parents. The difference is that they were able to realize that they had children for perhaps the wrong reasons but were then able to adjust to their new life and new responsibilities regardless.

When dysfunctional people have children for one of the reasons above, they are unable to learn from their mistakes and move on. They instead blame their resulting stress and unhappiness on the child. They decide that their child must be defective or intentionally "bad". They decide that the child inherited bad traits from their "no-good father" or "bitch mother". They become angry and resentful at the child for not living up to their standards and expectations. Once the parent has decided that about the child, there's nothing the child could ever do to fix the parent-child relationship or "prove themselves" to the parent.

After reading all of this, you may be left wondering "What's the right reason to have a child?" The right reason to have a child is because you have already found happiness and meaning in your life and feel ready to share that happiness with another person. You are ready and willing to give the time and energy necessary to raise a child in a loving and supportive home. You have no "needs" that you are looking for the child to fulfill. The only thing you want for your child is to be happy, in whatever path they choose for themselves.

Why my parent?

Like I said, not all parents are doomed to be dysfunctional just because they had children for the wrong reasons. But some parents are, and most of the time it is because they could be described as having been dysfunctional before they ever became parents. In cases like these the culprits are often untreated addiction or mental illness.

Let's start with addiction. Addiction can refer to alcohol or drug abuse or a process addiction. Process addictions include gambling addiction, sexual addiction, compulsive shopping, binge eating, etc. It is estimated that 9% of children in the United States live with a parent that is currently abusing drugs or alcohol (Substance Abuse and Mental Health Services Administration [SAMHSA], 2003). This does not include the children living with a parent with a process addiction such as gambling addiction. Either way we can assume that the total number of children living in a household with addiction is significant.

The nature of addiction is inherently dysfunctional and toxic. There is no logic to addiction. People engage in addictive behaviors essentially so that they can feel the way they did before they were addicted. If that last sentence didn't make sense to you, it is probably a good thing. In addition to this, when you are a parent who has an addiction, your children nor your family are your priorities. The addiction is your #1 priority. When the addiction takes hold of you, there is almost no limit a person will go to fulfill their addiction. Sadly, I have even heard from more than one client of their addicted parent trading sex with them to a pedophile for drugs.

Many addicted parents are abusive. Addicts, whether they are addicted to a substance or process, are naturally more depleted than non-addicted parents. The depletion is both simultaneously caused and temporarily alleviated by their "drug" of choice. As the addiction progresses, this depletion becomes more pronounced and apparent. The depletion that the parent feels is expressed outwardly as a person who lacks tolerance and does not handle frustrations well. Obviously those are not good traits for a parent as children require a great deal of both tolerance and patience. The children, whom are just being children, find themselves on the receiving end of their parent's frustration.

Neglect follows addiction. The addicted parent has a list of priorities where getting their next high is at the top of their list. Other things needed to maintain their addiction are next on their list. Their children are somewhere near the bottom of their list. The addict may think they're fooling everyone, but even the children know that they are not a priority.

When I was in Junior High I had a best friend named Rebecca. She was the oldest of four children and I really admired her for how smart she was and how well she did in school. Rebecca and I would have sleep-overs at her house like all pre-teen girls do. It was during these sleep-overs that I witnessed first-hand the neglect caused by and addicted parent. Rebecca was responsible for everything. She cooked dinner, she cleaned the house, and she did her best to keep her younger siblings in line. At some point her mother would stumble through the front door late at night, high on drugs, and then go straight to her bedroom and slam the bedroom door. She never said a word to anybody. I don't think she even realized I was there in her home. Her mother would then leave early in the morning to go to work. I was left wondering if she even ever spoke to her children. Rebecca had taken over as the parent of that household and was running the whole show herself. That's a lot of pressure for a 13 year old. They were the very definition of neglected children. Sadly her mother died a few years later of a drug over-dose.

Despite what the addict tells themselves, the children know they are not a priority for their addicted parents. The children are then left wondering what's so terrible about spending time with them that their parent won't do it. They wonder why their needs are always put last and determine that it is because their parent thinks that they are worthless. This then gets internalized and manifests as low self-esteem. Despite how much I admired Rebecca, she did not think highly of herself at all. When she entered High School she became promiscuous and started experimenting with her own drug use, eventually dropping out of school. The resulting low self- esteem and low self-confidence from having an addicted parent can last well into adulthood.

Another way that addiction negatively effects children are the "up's and downs" that accompany it. The children experience many false hopes during the course of their family member's addiction. The addicted family member swears that they can "use in moderation" or "have a handle on it" and for a while it appears that way. The person may even talk about going to AA or doing some other treatment. The children feel hopeful that this time it's for real, only to have their dreams dashed shortly afterwards. They will quickly cycle through hope and despair several times during the lifetime of the addict. Eventually the child grows pessimistic and cynical. They have no hope. They just feel angry.

Children derive a sense of stability through routine and structure. This is lost when you have an addicted parent as you never know what you will get on a day to day basis. Addiction naturally causes mood-swings and personality changes. For a child whom does not understand addiction, this can be very confusing and frightening. They may find that they never know which "dad" or "mom" they're going to get next.

The loss of stability that results from addiction in the family can also be said to be true when there is mental illness. Having one or both parents in the family be mentally ill is a strong contributor to family dysfunction. By its very definition, mental illness is dysfunctional. If it weren't, we would just say that the person is "quirky" or "thinks outside the box". It is when the person also has difficulty functioning that they cross the line from "different" to possibly being "mentally ill".

Of course, mental illness is by no means a life sentence! In my work as a therapist I've helped many people recover from mental illness. I've seen a great many people go on to have successful careers, be wonderful friends and partners, and be great parents. The difference I've noticed is that in dysfunctional families there is often a great aversion to getting treatment. The individual in question either says "There's nothing wrong with me!" or "Only the weak see a therapist and I'm not weak!"

On the flip side to this are family members who have been in therapy for years but have seemingly derived no benefit from it.

In general, people can only benefit from therapy if they are honest with the therapist. If you withhold information, lie about the things that are happening in your life, or in other ways try to make yourself look good to the therapist, you aren't going to benefit from therapy. Everybody knows that and it is for this reason that family members may come to suspect that the person is coning their therapist. They may announce their latest "break-through" in therapy only to have everyone else roll their eyes.

The mental illness in question may be severe such as bipolar disorder or schizophrenia, or it may be chronic as in an anxiety disorder or depression that never lifts. More often though in dysfunctional families we encounter family members with a mental illness that is vague and difficult to determine. You can tell there is something wrong with the person but you just can't put your finger on it. Whatever it is, it is pervasive and chronic. Although many people find that their mentally ill family member can act quite normal when the person has something to gain from it. Often to the outside world, they seem normal. People don't believe you when you tell them what goes on at home.

I'm going to address this more "vague" mental illness since it's the not knowing or not understanding that bothers people the most. When a family member is diagnosed with schizophrenia, it's devastating, but at least there's a name to the problem and a clear course of treatment. When nothing seems to fit or there's no name to the problem; that's something that really bothers people. If you read the previous paragraph and felt like I was describing your family member, it's possible that they may have something called a "personality disorder".

A personality disorder is a very serious diagnosis and is not a label to be put on someone casually. Early on in my career a supervisor told me that I should not diagnose a client with a personality disorder until I had been working with that client for at least a year. This is advice that I follow to this day. The diagnosis should really only be made by a mental health therapist because it is such a serious and difficult diagnosis to make.

What makes the diagnosis so difficult? For one, the disorder can look like something else at first and this is why people with personality disorders often have a history of having received several different diagnoses from therapists over the years. At first it can look like the person is just depressed or just has some anger issues. And because it is the nature of personality disorders to feel like everyone else is wrong, they may at first convince the therapist that that is in fact the case: that they don't have a problem and that it's their family's entire fault. Although most therapists do eventually catch on and realize that their client is perhaps more of the aggressor than the victim.

The symptoms of personality disorders can be described as both extreme and subtle. At times the person can appear very normal, while in their private life their behavior could be described as "insane" by those that know them best. This behavior can be so confusing to those around them that some people may start to question if they themselves are in fact crazy.

The thing that you need to understand about personality disorders is that for those whom are suffering with them, the world is a very confusing place. They have a hard time relating to other people and to them it seems like they are the only ones who really "get it". This causes them to come into conflict with other people often. The frustration of feeling like an alien in the world builds and then causes them to explode. They don't understand how their behavior affects other people, even their own family. To them, everyone else just seems so wrong and they don't understand why other people can't see that. This isn't to excuse their behavior, but understand that they truly believe that they are not doing anything wrong.

I'm not going to provide the diagnostic criteria for the various personality disorders as I feel that it is a diagnosis that should really only be made by a mental health professional and should not be made just by reading the criteria for diagnosis in a book. If you look up the criteria elsewhere and feel convinced that your family member does have a personality disorder, I should warn you that nothing will be gained by pointing that out to that family member. More than likely the person will become furious and you will regret having said it. I think it is also a cruel thing to do.

Personality disorders are very difficult to treat. There is no effective medication for a personality disorder and I doubt there ever will be. Progress in counseling is also often very slow. Typically it is something that will be with a person their entire lives. Change is not something that comes readily to the personality disordered, and you should be aware of that.

If you know that your family member has a personality disorder or merely suspect that they do or have some other enduring mental illness, you are probably wondering how this happened to them. Generally speaking, no one knows for sure why some people develop mental illness and others do not. There are a number of theories about it, but nothing has been proven. There is some research suggesting that mental illness is genetic. In other words, some people are just born that way. However, keep in mind that they are yet to identify the actual genetic mechanism responsible for mental illness. Researchers have merely noticed that mental illness seems to run in families. Until scientists are actually able to identify a gene or genetic process that causes mental illness, I remain highly skeptical that mental illness is caused by bad genes.

Another theory is that a trauma causes or triggers mental illness. This process seems clear: a person undergoes a traumatic event and they later develop Post Traumatic Stress Disorder (PTSD). But even this is unclear as research has revealed that actually most people who undergo a trauma do not develop PTSD (Iribarren, 2005). It would seem that it is the natural response of the brain to recover from trauma, even severe traumas.

Anecdotal evidence abounds of individuals who had difficult or traumatic childhoods who then went on to become fully functioning members of society. There is also plenty of anecdotal evidence of people who had difficult childhoods and that that then set on a trajectory course of lifelong depression, dysfunctional relationships, etc. Why do some have these experiences and develop mental illness while others do not? This is the question that continues to plague therapists. Some are even suggesting that the difference is due to head injuries in childhood (David, 2005; Mcallister, 2010). Proponents of this theory claim that head injuries need not be severe enough to cause a concussion or unconsciousness in the victim in order to trigger mental illness.

When it comes to personality disorders, it would seem that the seeds for the illness are sown early in life. One of the prevailing theories of where personality disorders come from is that they develop as a result of growing up in a dysfunctional family (Allen, 2010; Rosenberg, 2013). The prevailing theory is that the individual develops these dysfunctional behaviors as a way to survive amongst the chaos. For instance, a person with Paranoid Personality Disorder may have grown up in a family where everybody really was out to get them! It was good for them to always be on guard and questioning other people's motives. At that time, the behaviors were very helpful to them, however as they grew up and left the family the behaviors no longer work for them. Instead of helping them survive, they now only cause problems.

But once again, growing up in a dysfunctional family does not doom a person to have a personality disorder. There are plenty of people who grow up in dysfunctional families and have no mental illness. There are also plenty of people with personality disorders that came from normal families. Psychology does not yet know what causes mental illness or personality disorders in particular.

The truth is, there are a lot of things about your family that you will never know or understand. Instead, all we can do is to try to see our family for who they really are and accept that we are not capable of changing them.

The hallmarks of dysfunctional families

Even if you are never able to find the answers for why your family is the way it is, it can help to understand that you are not alone. Dysfunctional families, despite having very different origins and cultures, do share a lot of the same patterns and characteristics. Recognizing the hallmarks of dysfunctional families can give you a better understand of how your family "works" as well as reaffirm to yourself that you were not the cause of this behavior.

- **Blame:** I say "parent" in a lot of these, but really these descriptors can refer to any dysfunctional family member or just the entire family in general. It is just in my experience that it is usually a parent or step-parent that is the primary aggressor. That being said, blame is a hallmark of dysfunctional families. There typically are certain family members that are "blameless" no matter what they do while there are other family members that consistently take the fall. The blameless essentially get a free pass to do whatever they want and often take advantage of the situation. The blamed eventually stop trying to defend themselves and just absorb all of the blame. They eventually internalize this blame and may grow up to be adults that feel very much responsible for the feelings and actions of other people.
- **Lack of personal responsibility:** With the exception of "the blamed", there is a lack of personal responsibility, especially when it comes to the parents or the aggressors in the family. This lack of personal responsibility often goes to the extreme where the person in question will not take responsibility for absolutely anything. If they knock over a drink then it's your fault for having bought those glasses that knock over easily. Even if you directly confront the person and have evidence that they are in fact to blame, the person will still find a way to deny responsibility. You will never be able to convince them that they are wrong.
- **Selective memory:** This lack of responsibility and blamelessness can also manifest in the form of selective memory. It is not at all uncommon for the aggressor to claim to have no memory of the event in question or to

simply say it never happened. This may also manifest itself in the person claiming to have "blackouts" when they get angry. Their argument is that you made them so angry that they "blacked-out" and thus have no memory of what they did nor should they be held responsible for whatever they did during the "blackout". You should know that there is no evidence for anger-induced blackouts. There is evidence for alcohol-induced blackouts where a person drinks so much that the part of the brain responsible for forming memories actually ceases to work. There is no evidence that anger could be so intense as to stop certain parts of the brain from working, nor should black-outs be used as an excuse even if it were true. The angry person should take responsibility for their anger and leave the anger-inducing situation long before it ever reaches the point of blacking-out and losing control.

- **Restricted range of emotion:** In dysfunctional families it is not at all unusual for certain emotions or the expression of those emotions to not be "okay". The parent doesn't have to express this directly as it can also just be implied through the parent's reactions to these emotions or to the "punishments" that follow them. A number of clients have expressed to me that it was not allowed for them to feel sad in their family. Despite all of the torment they experienced on a daily basis, they could not cry about it or express sadness for the way they were treated. If they did, family members yelled at them, hit them, or turned away from them in disgust.

- **Hypocrisy:** I suppose that there is some degree of hypocrisy in every parent-child relationship, however, in dysfunctional families it is far more pronounced. The way hypocrisy manifests itself most often is through a parent who says "Do as I say, not as I do". The parent breaks all the rules but you are just supposed to ignore all of that. It may also take the form of their being different rules for different children. Of course, there are naturally different expectations depending on the age of the child. That's not what I'm talking about here. In dysfunctional families, even when you take age into consideration, things are still unequal and unfair. One child may get extra-special privileges or often go without punishment when they misbehave. When one child complains about being abused by a sibling and not being allowed to fight back, the parent scolds "You have to be the better one!" Hypocrisy can also manifest itself between siblings. For instance, you may have an older brother who gets angry with you if you do the slightest thing, but expects you to just take whatever abuse he dishes out.

- **Lack of privacy:** Within the family, there is very little privacy. Family members walk-in on each other while they are in the bathroom or changing their clothes. Parents will often read their children's diaries and ridicule the child about what they wrote in front of the rest of the family. It may be against the rules to shut or lock bedroom doors. It is also not unheard of to have the parents of these families actually remove their child's bedroom door off the hinges. One client disclosed to me that growing up all of the doors in her home had glass panels so that one could see into the room. This even included the bathroom door. This lack of privacy is sometimes a precursor to sexual abuse in the home. The predator insists on this lack of privacy because it allows them easier access to the children in the home.

- **Extreme privacy:** This is usually only in regards to outside of the home. Inside the home there are almost no boundaries, but when it comes to outside the home the parent will insist that the child uphold the strictest boundaries with those outside of the family. This often means forcing the child to keep "secrets" about the family. The child is not allowed to discuss anything about the family with outsiders; not even the jobs that the parents have or the neighborhood they live in. Sleep-overs and having friends over is also often off-limits.

- **Disowned family:** During your childhood, one or more family members may have been disowned by the family. This may have happened before you were born or some-time during your childhood. Once children realize that certain family members have been disowned, it can make their own safety and security within the family feel tenuous. Children may wonder "Am I next?" Children may become fearful to speak their minds to their parents or in other ways be themselves, afraid that a wrong move could send them out the door.

- **Controlling:** In general, the family or certain family members are very controlling of you. This may mean controlling who you can be friends with, whom you can be in a relationship with, or what career you choose. I remember one 17 year old client whose curfew was 4pm. If she was not home by 4pm her mother would call the police on her. The girl was only allowed to leave the home if she was going to school or therapy.

- **Critical:** Within the family there is a lot of criticism. You are not allowed to fail or have an "off-day". Anything less than perfection is met with criticism or berating. At the same time, there is little to praise if you do accomplish something. There may also be inequitable treatment where one person receives nothing but criticism while another person is appeased and placated.

- **Jealousy:** Jealousy within dysfunctional families can manifest itself in a few different ways. One way is that you may find that your family becomes strangely jealous when you spend time with friends or significant others. One parent may become jealous when you spend time with your other parent. Basically, you feel like the family wants you all to themselves and you feel pulled in many different directions. Cancelling a family get-together is then followed by days, perhaps even years, of guilt-tripping. They may even seek to manipulate you by threatening or implying suicide if you don't spend time with them. Another way jealousy manifests itself is when the family becomes jealous or resentful of your accomplishments. This is often confusing to the person subjected to it because seemingly their whole life their family has been telling them that they were never good enough, now they find themselves in a position of being "too good". Rather than celebrate your success, you get the impression that your family doesn't want to see you happy.

Conclusion

Like all families, dysfunctional families start with someone deciding to bring a child into the world. However, rather than be raised in a healthy and warm family, the child finds themselves being raised in a family that is cold, critical, controlling, and abusive. The child is often singled-out and subjected to unfair treatment. Naturally, as children do, they grow to blame themselves for the way they are treated and decide that it is acceptable behavior for them to be abused by other people.

But at some point, probably in adulthood, you started to question if it was really just you. Maybe you aren't the bad one after all. Maybe it was in fact your family that was bad. Maybe you are just the product of a toxic family. As you start to put the pieces together and realize that things were not normal in your family, you're left wondering why. Why did they act the way they did? Why do they still treat me like I'm 12 years old? Where did the dysfunction come from?

Hopefully reading this chapter allowed you to get some answers. Perhaps it spurred you to contact one or more family members and ask them about some of things you've read so far. Hopefully you found the conversation to be helpful. One of the things that you have to accept though is that you will never have all of the answers. No one will ever know exactly why and where things went wrong. Especially if you try to confront the person who was the most abusive towards you, it is unlikely that they will be able to give a rational explanation for why they acted the way that they did.

Part of healing is accepting that you'll never fully understand it. To use a tired old cliché: *It is what it is.* That of course doesn't mean that you have to continue being abused or mistreated in your life. I'm going to give you some clear instructions regarding how you can take your life back. But before we get into that, I'm going to devote the next two chapters of this book towards helping you to gain a better understanding of your parent's actions and then later your sibling's behavior towards you.

2

The one who's supposed to protect you the most

Anita was the youngest of three. She had two older brothers. On the outside, she seemed to have a picture perfect life. The children lived in a nice house in the suburbs where they each got to have their own bedroom. Her parents would participate in the community and were well-liked. All of the children got good grades in school and Anita's brother was even in a gifted program. However, within the privacy of the home, things were very different.

Her parents were married, but unhappily. They would fight almost every night, and sometimes the fights got physical. It was not uncommon for Anita to go to sleep to the sounds of yelling, banging, and shattered glass. Her parents often fought about money. Anita's father had a gambling addiction and the money it took to fuel his addiction was substantial. The mortgage and other essentials were often at risk of not being paid. The gambling addiction meant that the children couldn't have extras like money for ordering a pizza, going on a school field trip, or having new clothes. Compared to the other children in their neighborhood, they went without, and Anita and her brothers knew this.

Early on, Anita learned that it was better not to ask for anything. If she did ask for something, her mother would become so angry that it was almost like she was possessed. Her face would turn red and twisted with rage. It scared Anita. Oddly enough this would not scare her brothers, who would rage back until their mother gave in or they would simply take the money out of her purse. Anita's mother had no control over the boys. The boys ruled the house and the mother gave up trying to parent them. However, it was a different story when Anita's father was around. The boys were afraid of him and he could be quite harsh. He demanded perfect grades and perfect behavior from his children. Anita never felt like she measured up to her father's expectations, although she always tried her best to please him.

As much as he demanded from his children, Anita's father was far from perfect himself. He would disappear for days, sometimes weeks. It got to the point where he was gambling away his whole paycheck. To make up for this, he started committing fraud and embezzling money from work. As time went on, he became bolder with the amount of money he stole. His brashness was his downfall, as it eventually led to him being caught. From the time he was charged with embezzlement until he went to jail, Anita's father's behavior became increasingly violent and scary. Anita's mother decided enough was enough and divorced him.

It was a bitter divorce. At one point, Anita's father threatened to kill her mother and she believed that he would do it if given the chance. There was even a break-in one night, and Anita's mother was convinced that her husband had broken into the house to try to scare them. Anita feared that if they had been home that night that he may have killed her mom. He continued to stalk and threaten them until he went to jail. It was a very scary time for Anita.

They moved to a tiny apartment in a bad part of town. Anita's mother worked as much as she could and most of the time there was no adult supervision. Anita's brothers' behavior worsened after the divorce. Her oldest brother seemed to take dad's role of being the big and scary one. He terrorized her. One day he choked her to the point where she blacked out. She was truly afraid that one day he would kill her.

Her middle brother, instead of defending her, would often join in. He discovered that it was safer to be friends with the older brother than be the object of his torment. He also found that he could easily manipulate his brother as well as his mother. Sometimes Anita would even fall for his cons, so desperate to have *someone on her side. Her older brother exploited and used her too. No matter how hard she tried to make herself invisible, both brothers stole from her, physically abused her, and teased her relentlessly.*

When Anita tried to explain to her mom what was happening at home, her mother would become angry with her and mock her by saying "Oh! Poor little victim girl!" When Anita got upset that her mother would say this, her mother would continue to mock her by saying "Go run away and cry then, little victim girl!" Anita's mother would only do something about her sons' behavior if it affected her, such as them stealing money from her purse or talking back. She didn't seem to care that they were doing much worse to Anita on a daily basis. Anita got no sympathy from her mother.

Her childhood was Hell. She had no friends and no safe place she could ever turn to. She was in constant fear of what was going to happen next. Why wouldn't her mother take her torment seriously? Why would she mock her like that? Why would she do nothing to protect her from her brothers? It was as if she was too selfish to care that her daughter was suffering.

Anita often struggled with a love/hate relationship with her mother, which continued even into adulthood. She knew that in a lot of ways her mother was a victim too. Although her mother did not physically abuse her, she wondered if what she experienced could be considered emotional abuse or neglect. Even though her brothers were the primary abusers, she felt anger that her mother never did anything to protect her.

In this chapter, I'm going to be addressing parents and their role in the dysfunctional family. Every family consists of a parent or parental figure. You may have been raised with both biological parents in the home like Anita was, you may have had a single parent household like Joe, or you may have been raised in the foster care system or by a relative such as a grandparent. Either way, we all had someone in our lives that fit the role of "parent".

We look to that person as the one who we should be able to depend on the most. The one we can rely on more than anyone else. The one who loves us the most. The one who is supposed to protect us the most. This is why it is especially painful when they also abuse us. They may not have physically abused you, but failure to protect you from abuse is also abuse. Mocking your pain, like Anita's mother did, is certainly emotional abuse.

Your parent is still your parent

One of the hardest things to reconcile as an adult child of a dysfunctional family is that your parent played a key part in your torment. Even if your parents never abused you directly, if they knew that abuse was going on but didn't stop it, they were instruments in that abuse. When you're a child, you rely on your parent for absolutely everything. If you were being abused, you didn't have the power to protect yourself, but they did. Like Anita, you probably have a lot of anger regarding their failure to protect you. It may then be hard for other people to understand why you still try so hard to have a relationship with them.

Before I was in private practice, I worked at a community counseling center where a lot of my clients were adult children of dysfunctional families. Although they were fully grown, had their own families and their own lives, they were still very much under the thumb of their toxic parent. Their parent could no longer physically beat them as their child was now of an age and size where they could easily over-power them if they tried, but the parent could certainly continue to emotionally abuse them and control them through guilt. The parent would demand that their adult child take them to various appointments and shopping trips even though they were perfectly capable of doing so themselves. Their parent called them incessantly about different things they needed from them. While their adult child was doing those favors they would criticize and berate them the whole time, all while their adult child meekly followed orders. Although these were fully grown adults, they were still treated almost the same way as when they were children.

I went to my supervisor and told her about the situation so many of my clients were in. I asked her why they didn't just stop picking up the phone when their abusive parent called. To me, it seemed that all they had to do was stop answering their phone calls and the problem would be solved. My supervisor paused, and then answered "Your parent is still your parent." It doesn't matter how abusive a person is to you, they are still your parent and always will be. They will still have an important place in your life and it isn't easy to just let go of that.

So many adults of abusive parents have a love/hate relationship with their parents. They love them because they are their parent. They love the idea of having a "mom" or having a "dad". However, they hate the reality of their situation.

For an adult child of a dysfunctional family, it can be painful to see the relationship their peers have with their parents. For instance, at your college graduation you see how other students' families cheered and got genuinely excited for their child's achievement. Meanwhile yours just sat there looking bored or complaining about the heat. Your friends tell you how their mom is their best friend, but you know that if you ever were to try to go to your mom for advice she would just criticize you or give you a strange look that seems to communicate "Why are you coming to me for this?" You know that for most people, if the going gets tough they can always fall back on their parents. You have no one to fall back on. Or perhaps they would help you, but they'd never let you forget about it.

Although objectively and rationally you know that your parents aren't like other people's parents, you can't let go of the hope that they someday will be. Every time you interact with them you think "Maybe today will be the day." Maybe this time you'll be able to please them. Maybe this time you'll prove yourself to them. Maybe this time they'll realize how unfair they've been to you and want to change. Maybe this time it'll be different. But it never is.

In the end it's always a disappointment. Even if your parent seems to be doing "good" for a while, eventually the pendant swings back in the other direction and they show their true selves once more. Other people get frustrated by it. Your spouse complains about your parent's behavior and at the very least wants you to stop doing special favors for them. You feel torn because despite how cruel your parent is to you, you still love them.

You love them for the simple fact that they are your parent and there may have been some special nurturing moments for you when you were little that you just can't ignore. The parent-child bond is very strong and it takes a lot for it to be severed. Your family also loves to remind you that "You only get one mother" and "Your dad's not going to be around forever you know." You feel guilty about setting limits with them and worry that you will one day regret these limits when the time comes that your parents eventually pass away. In addition to this, there may be another reason why you continue to hold on.

From a very young age you were trained to believe that your very being depended on your relationship with your parents. Now certainly, when we are very young, our lives really do depend on our parents. This is true for all young children. Until a certain age, we can't do anything for ourselves. We rely on our parents to feed us, bathe us, put us to sleep, and to communicate to others if there is something wrong because we can't even speak for ourselves. As we get older, we develop these skills and gradually take over from our parents. However, I have noticed in dysfunctional families that the parents act as though it is in their best interests to keep their children helpless and dependent on them. After all, if their children were to become independent and self-sufficient, they would be able to live their own lives and that would threaten the whole equation.

These parents repeatedly give their children the message, either overtly or covertly, that they can't survive on their own: that they are not responsible enough to have their own cell-phone plan; that they have weak personalities others will exploit; that they will die of loneliness without their adult child living with them; that the neighbors will talk about what an ungrateful child you are. And most importantly, they are often given the message that there is no safety net. The message is "Once you step out on your own, that's it! Don't expect any help from me!" This is scary for a young person that has been being controlled their whole life.

The threat to you may not necessarily be to your survival, but rather to your self-worth as a person. It has also been drilled into your head that your self-esteem depends on their approval of you. Without them in your life it may feel like you have nothing left to live for. And that's why it's so hard to take yourself out the equation, because you believe that without them your very being is at risk. But there's still hope!

Understanding the equation

By now, you understand that there is a role that you fit into in your family and that that role is part of a larger equation. In non-dysfunctional families, children also often have roles. The difference is that in normal families, the children choose their roles and the roles are neither harmful nor more favored than any other child's in the family. For instance, in a normal family you may find that one brother takes on the role of "the athletic one" and the other brother takes on the role of "the artistic one". For both children, these roles are a source of pride and provide them with experiences of mastery.

In dysfunctional families, children are either assigned roles by their parents or forced into certain roles by a dysfunctional family system. The roles are negative and prevent the children from living authentically. Something that's important to remember is that the equation always starts with the parents. They either create it themselves or in some other way enable it to exist. Most likely, you already knew that. The thing you probably don't understand is why your parents do this in the first place. To understand this, we need to understand how they think.

Your parents don't view families and children the way that normal parents do. Part of it may be that they are just repeating the same dysfunctional behaviors that they observed from their own parents, but I believe that it takes a bit more than just that. In general, your parents have very different beliefs about the way that a family works. These beliefs are very concrete and not easily changed.

Not every dysfunctional parent is going to have the same set of beliefs, but I will list the most common ones. Hopefully one of these will ring true for you and help you to gain a better understanding of the way your parent thinks this way and why they act the way they do.

- **"Children are possessions"**: The parent very much views their children as being theirs. They created you, therefor they own you. You cannot make your own decisions because you are not your own person. You are an extension of them. This can reach an extreme where because you are the parent's possession, they feel it is perfectly acceptable for them to have access to your body. A sexually abusive parent may even give you the excuse that what they are doing to you isn't wrong because you are "their blood" and "they made you". Part of this may be that your parent has an extreme entitlement complex. They feel entitled to your company, your time, your money, and perhaps even your body. Another possibility is that they are simply possessive. They had a child because they wanted to be able to say that they had something that was theirs; something that nobody could take away from them. Because they view their children as their possessions; how dare you have an opinion? How dare you make a reasonable request to be treated with respect? How dare you make your own decisions? How dare you try to pull away from them? They made you, therefore they own you.
- **"Children fulfill my needs"**: Children have needs. Parents have needs. We all have needs. The problem is when

parents use their children to fulfill their needs. Toxic parents often don't understand that the parent-child relationship is one sided. This is partly what makes it so dysfunctional, by definition it doesn't function. Children need their parents. Even in adulthood, adult children turn to their parents for advice, venting, and to fulfill other emotional needs. These parents don't understand that it is not right to then have a give-and-take with their children. They feel that it is "only fair" that after changing all those diapers and listening to toddlers whine about toys, that they then get to do their own "unloading" and whining too. I have heard of parents using children as young as five as their own personal therapists. Nothing is off the table: They complain to their children about their sex lives, the affair they are having, their suspicions that their spouse is having an affair, viciously complaining about the other parent, and venting about money problems. This type of behavior has been referred to as "emotional incest". You may feel that the term is too severe, but keep in mind that this "venting" puts a lot of stress on children. To the child listening to this information, it seems that the very livelihood of the family is in danger of falling apart any second. For a child, you might as well tell them that the world is going to end. It's a tremendous burden to put on a child who does not have the maturity to understand the situation nor the ability to do anything about it. In addition to emotional needs, the parent may see children as existing to fulfill their financial needs. These parents often see their children as their "retirement". They fully expect to be moving in with one of them when they are old and thus feel no need to have any kind of retirement savings or plan. Although I think it's a good thing for children to have chores, a dysfunctional parent may have their children do <u>all</u> of the chores, while they do nothing but relax. Once their children reach working age, they may see their children's paychecks as a means to supplement their own irresponsible lifestyle. I have heard of many instances of dysfunctional parents spending all of their child's college fund or grandparent's inheritance without any thought that their child may have a right or ownership of that money. To them, the concept of their child having their own needs, or that the relationship would be more to the child's benefit and not the parent's, is ridiculous.

- **"As the parent, I choose their fate":** Again, in functional families, children choose roles and paths in life that are authentic to them. In dysfunctional families, children are not given that option. The parent makes the choice for them. It's not so much that the parent feels uniquely qualified to make life decisions for their child, although they may use that excuse, it's more that they simply feel entitled to. You see, before you were born, your parent planned out your entire life. *They decided that as a child you would play these types of games and be interested in these types of things and have these types of friends. As an adult you would go to this college, have this career, and marry this type of spouse.* That was their fantasy and they did everything in their power to try to mold you into that fantasy. This type of behavior comes from a parent that is deeply dissatisfied with their own life and their own accomplishments. For whatever reason, they felt incapable of living out that fantasy themselves, so to them the next best thing was to have a child and then have that child do it for them. Because they feel that they sacrificed their own dreams for you, for you to then try to do something else with your life is devastating to them. In a way, it threatens their whole existence. They feel that their life will be meaningless if you don't live out that fantasy for them. In their mind, it would be like they had lived a failed life. That is why they become so enraged when you try to live out your own dreams.
- **"Children should be grateful":** The dysfunctional parent feels that because they gave you life, you should be grateful

for whatever treatment you get from them. They feel that children should always be grateful to their parents, and thus they become enraged if you even hint that they are mistreating you. A good example of this would be Anita's mother from the beginning of this chapter. Anita's father definitely had the philosophy that his children were his possessions, he decided their fate, and that they existed to fulfill his needs. Anita's mother did not seem to have the same philosophy of her ex-husband, but she did believe that children should be grateful. That is why she became angry when Anita asked for money, because if her mind she felt that Anita should be grateful for what she already had. The idea that Anita would want to have as much as other kids angered her because she saw it as spoiled behavior. She also became angry when Anita complained about her brothers' treatment of her because she felt that Anita was being ungrateful for her life by complaining. What Anita's mother doesn't understand is that children should not have to be grateful for basic things like a nice home to live in, clean clothes, and a safe environment. Children should be entitled to those things.

- **"Children raise themselves"**: In the age of helicopter parenting and overly-attached parents, this type of thinking may come across as unusual. It is often the case that dysfunctional parents are overly-controlling, but it is not always so. Sometimes they are very lax in their parenting style to the point of neglect. In their minds, their only responsibility is to provide a home for their children to live in and to keep the pantry full of food. Some parents don't feel that they need to do even that, that perhaps children are also capable of foraging for their own food. They go off to work (or just go off!) and the children fend for themselves. The children have very little parental supervision and the parent does not see a problem with this. The problem is that there are people in society (some of which may be your very own relatives) who prey on children who do not have parental supervision. If you think about it, it does make sense from a predator's point of view. To a predator, this is a golden opportunity. Savvy adults can often spot a predator a mile away, and thus keep their children away from them, but children with no parental supervision just see the predator as someone "cool" who has taken an interest in them. When these children are then exploited by the predator, they feel they have no one to turn to or their parent simply doesn't want to deal with it.

It is because your parent has one or more of these beliefs that they act the ways they do. It is very unlikely that they will ever change these beliefs no matter how inaccurate or dysfunctional they are. The good news is that they don't actually have to change these beliefs in order for you take yourself out of the equation. You can change the equation with or without their agreement. We'll talk more about that later. For now, I want to go into further detail about the long term effects on you of having an abusive or enabling parent.

Like a curse

Every year, reports are made to Child Protective Services that more than 6 million children are abused by their parents (U.S. Dept. of Health & Human Services, 2012). But what about the cases that don't get reported? It is very likely that your own abuse was never reported to anyone. Your family was able to hide the dysfunction to the public and because of that, no one noticed. It is because of this that I think that the actual statistic of the number of children being abused by their own parents is actually much, much higher.

Child abuse is still very much a quiet and unsympathized plight for children in these situations. To some, that last sentence may come across as shocking. Many people would like to believe that if anything, we can all agree that children should not be abused, and that anyone would fight to ensure a child's right to live in a safe and loving home. After all, aren't politicians always rallying behind statements about child welfare and how they are our future and all that? You would think that would be the case, but I have found that more often than not actions do not follow words when it comes to keeping children safe.

Before I was in private practice, I worked at an agency whose primary clientele were abused children. I worked as a therapist with children who had undergone trauma so severe at the hands of their own parents that most people couldn't even imagine it. The traumas were worse than anything I had ever seen depicted in any movie or read in any book. As horrible as this abuse was, in just about every case there was at least one (often more) rational adult who knew what was going on in that family but never stepped in to protect the children. In some cases, it was even government agencies and institutions that had failed to do anything about it.

Even in this day and age, children who step forward and tell an adult about their abuse are told that they are lying, labeled as a "trouble-maker", or seen as a brat that perhaps brought the abuse on themselves by being so insufferable. One of my clients wasn't able to get authorities to believe that she was being raped by her father until she was able to produce a video of the abuse. The big reward you get if someone actually believes you is you are put in foster care. One statistic cites that 28% of children are abused while in foster care. Again, I believe that the actual number is probably much higher than that, but if we were to take these government statistics at face value, then that still means that there are more children being abused in foster care than anywhere else. And remember, foster care is where we put abused children so that they can be "safe".

These children know all about the foster care system. They've heard horror stories on the news, from other kids at school, and probably from their own parents. Abusive parents often threaten their children "And if you tell someone they'll put you in a foster home!" This is not to say that all foster parents are bad.

During my work as a therapist I've met some really great ones who became foster parents because they wanted to make the world a better place. But you must understand that to an abused child, the prospect of going to foster care often seems like a worse fate than staying in their dysfunctional family. In their minds, when it comes to their own families, at least they know what to expect. They have no clue what to expect from a foster parent or what abuse awaits them. And it is because these children seemingly have no good options that they often don't tell anyone and choose to remain in the abusive household.

The point is that there are a lot of children being abused by their parents and most don't get any help. And even for the ones who do get help, most of the time that help isn't great. When you get abused by the one that is supposed to love and protect you the most, how do you think a child rationalizes that? So many children decide that they must be so unlovable and so horrible as to deserve it.

In psychology, it is recognized that people have certain biases in their thinking. One such bias is called "The Just World Bias". To sum it up, the just world bias states that good things happen to good people and bad things happen to bad people. This is the same phenomenon that causes people to often think that victims of crime somehow brought the misfortune onto themselves by being foolish or in some way "asking for it". What do you think happens when a child has this same belief? The child decides that if bad things happen to bad people, then they must be bad; they must somehow deserve their abuse. I have seen this belief system over and over again in abused children. As a therapist who now only works with adult clients, I have also seen this belief frequently in adults who come from dysfunctional families.

When you are abused by your own parent, or your abuse is in some way allowed by your parent, a person doesn't know how to think of that other than that they in some way must deserve it. You add to this the fact that there are many other people who know about the abuse but don't do anything about it and the belief is strengthened. Also add to this that so many times there are people actually telling the person that yes they deserved the abuse, and well, what do you expect the person to think?

The long term effect of having this kind of belief about yourself is devastating. When a person believes that they deserved the abuse they suffered, it affects the way they behave around other people, not just the parent or the abuser. They frequently grow up to be people who can't stand up for themselves, who accept mistreatment from other people, and go on to be victimized again and again throughout their lives.

Their fearfulness and meekness make them an easy target for bullies when they are in school. The thing you have to understand about bullies is that they go after easy targets. It has nothing to do with whether they believe that their victim deserves to be bullied or not. They are merely targeting someone that they think will take it. Typically this is someone who is not surrounded by friends that could defend them and someone that they feel would neither fight back nor tell anyone about the abuse; someone who will keep quiet about the bullying. It is because of that, that children who are abused at home are often bullied at school also.

Of course, it's important to note that the bully and the bullied come from the same types of homes. Yes, typically they both come from dysfunctional families and broken homes. The bully just deals with it differently. They get a sense of mastery in their life by over-powering helpless opponents, not unlike how the adults in their home over-power them. As someone who has been a therapist for both bullies and the bullied, I can tell you that they are shockingly similar. It's too bad that none of them realized this while they were both in school together.

Back to the bullied: So they are not only abused at home, but also at school. In bullying situations, you have to understand that there are often several collaterals. It's not just the one bully and the victim. When a bullying situation occurs, there are often several other children who see an opportunity and join in with the bully, or at least watch and laugh. There are also teachers who know what's going on and don't do anything about it. So now to the child it feels not just that they are bullied, but that perhaps everyone in the whole school hates them, and they have no idea why.

They are hated at home and hated at school. As I mentioned earlier, there are people in our society that prey on vulnerable individuals. These predators are often adults but also children and can be found outside of school and outside of the home. As the child's self-esteem degrades further, they become an ever-more tempting target to the people that prey on people like them. Soon, it becomes apparent to the child that they are mistreated just about everywhere they go and no one seems to care. *Maybe I really do deserve this?*

These experiences of being almost constantly rejected and mistreated are painful. Because we all just want to live the most painless life possible, it prompts the child to do some soul-searching. They decide that there must be something about them that is so horrible or so off-putting to other people that it invites this kind of treatment from other people. *What is it about me that cause other people to treat me this way?* They think and think and think but they can't figure it out. In the end they determine that there is just something about them that turns other people off; they are inherently unworthy as a person. They don't know what it is exactly, but it's something. It's like a curse. They are cursed to be mistreated by other people.

Of course, you are not cursed and you do not deserve to be mistreated, ever. You are treated the way you are because you have been forced into an equation where your role is to be the mistreated one. The problem is that this equation doesn't just exist within your dysfunctional family. It often follows you to school, later to your place of employment, and finally in your relationships with other adults.

I've often wondered if other people can somehow tell that we come from dysfunctional families, what our roles in those families were specifically, and then continue to place us in those roles. Other people certainly treat us as if they know this information about us. There is evidence in psychology that people can determine a shockingly accurate and large amount of information about who we are as people just by looking at us. Perhaps other kids at school can tell that someone is the Golden Child at home and then they too put that person on a pedestal. Perhaps our employer can somehow sense a person is the Invisible Child and so also chooses to ignore them come promotion time. Another possibility is that we pick up patterns of behavior from years of being abused and that these subtle behaviors give us away.

Years of abuse by your parent and subsequent others lead to some bad habits. Let's take a moment to examine these bad habits that abused children develop and then keep in adulthood. Recognizing these habits and understanding where they come from is the first step in ending them for good.

The false self

One of these bad habits is that you create a "false self" in order to protect yourself. You decide that the real you is unacceptable to other people so naturally you create a false you that you think will be more pleasing to others. This false self can manifest itself in a few different ways. You may find that you do all of these or just one of these.

One of the ways that we create a false self is that we become really good at reading other people. Remember how I said that psychology has shown that people can tell a lot about you just by looking at you? Well, that ability goes both ways. You gain the ability to quickly assess what other people want from you and you instantly set about to become that person. You mold yourself to different people and different situations. The term often used for such a person is a "social chameleon".

The problem with such an approach is that it often means that you cannot spend time with different friends at the same time because different friends each know a different you. So you do your best to keep these people separate. You may even run in to the problem where you forget which "you" you are supposed to be with someone. One client told me about a time where she forgot which persona she was supposed to be with a certain coworker. She ended up using the wrong persona and the coworker was quite alarmed by the experience of seeing a very different version of her. The coworker avoided her after that.

Another problem with being a social chameleon is that relationships tend to stay superficial. You find that you have many great acquaintances but no true friends. This is because friendship requires a certain amount of authenticity, trust, and intimacy in order to develop. When you are a social chameleon, you have none of those things. After a while, you may even get to the point where you no longer know who the real you is anymore.

Another way that we create a false self is through lying. Lying is a natural consequence of being abused by a parent. When it seems like no matter what we do it's never good enough, we quickly learn that lying is a possible way to "cheat the system". If any flaw or mistake (and we all have flaws and we all make mistakes at least once per day) results in a harsh punishment, we learn that lying may be a way to avoid that punishment.

Lying may also be seen as a way of making ourselves more acceptable to other people. Remember, the message you repeatedly got growing up was that who you are isn't good enough, so sometimes people resort to lying to make themselves seem better. One client of mine got tired of hearing about all of the cool things other kids were doing with their families. Those families had money to go on family vacations or other adventures. His parents didn't have money because his father was always blowing it on failed investment schemes. So he started lying about the amazing trips he went on and places he had seen. In reality he had never gone anywhere, but other children were impressed with his stories.

Once you have a few successful experiences with lying, it becomes self-reinforcing, almost addictive in nature. You start lying more and more. After a while you start lying about things you have no reason to lie about. You're lying without even thinking. Lies just fly out of your mouth and you wonder "Why did I lie about that?" You wish you could stop lying but it's like a really bad habit that you can't control. You worry that your lies are going to catch up with you and people are going to figure it out, if they haven't already. The resulting feelings of insecurity obviously don't help, as it was insecurity that caused you to lie in the first place.

Another way that people create a false self is that they create a "tough" persona. They look to the abusers in their life and say to themselves "Dad's so big and scary. Nobody messes with dad. I'm going to be like dad!" So they take on the characteristics of the abuser. They decide that it's a dog-eat-dog world. You're either the abuser or the victim and they don't want to be the victim anymore. There are some people that the only way they can feel up is by making other people feel down, so they abuse their siblings and bully other kids at school.

The bully persona is so convincing that other people don't see the truth. As a therapist, I've been a therapist to both bullies and the bullied. The surprising thing I've learned from this experience is that the bullied are actually emotionally stronger than the bullies themselves. Once they take down their bully persona you see that the person underneath is incredibly emotionally fragile. They fall apart at the blink of an eye. They are very wounded people, often more wounded than their victims.

The bullies, at least the ones that end up in therapy, often express to me a desire to not be a bully anymore. The problem is that they don't know what else to do. They have so much built up rage within themselves that it only causes a slight annoyance for them to fly off the handle. They feel especially disgusted by people who remind them of their true selves: the abused meek individual. In attacking that person, it is almost like they are trying to destroy that part of themselves that they hate. And that is why they feel so much satisfaction in the moment and have such a hard time stopping themselves from doing it again.

This false self is a natural consequence of having been abused by your family. Although at the moment you feel at a loss as to how to stop it, there is hope. You can destroy your false self by abandoning it and embracing your authentic self. I'll go into more detail about how to do that later.

Conclusion

You may feel that your parent was not the aggressor in your dysfunctional family. Perhaps it was a sibling, a toxic grandparent, or mom's boyfriend. Whether your parent directly abused you or not, it is my belief that a parent's inability to protect their child from abuse also constitutes abuse. Enabling abuse or turning a blind eye to a child in distress is abuse. More than anyone, our parents are supposed to protect us, and when they fail to, it is abuse. This is not just my opinion, but also the opinion of Child Protective Services and the Court system.

When we are abused by our parents, whether directly or indirectly, it changes who we are as people. We decide that we deserve to be mistreated by others and set out on a path of continuous exploitation by other people. We get into dysfunctional relationships, we are mistreated and taken advantage of at work, and perhaps we even go on to mistreat others. Because we are given the message that who we are isn't good enough or isn't worthy, we create a false self. We lose who we are as people.

3

Sibling rivalry or sibling abuse?

Mark was the younger of two boys. He grew up in suburbia with his older brother Eric. Their parents had them later in life and both worked as High School teachers. Mark's parents were both good church-going people. Their only flaw was that they were both extremely reserved and somewhat socially inept. Mark took after his parents: reserved, quiet, shy, introverted, and somewhat nerdy. But when it came to his brother, it was almost as if Eric came from a different family. He was athletic, handsome, extroverted, and socially very charming. He played football in High School and took martial arts for years. He always had a girlfriend. It was obvious to Mark that his parents admired Eric. Eric represented the life they had always wanted for themselves but never had.

Mark's parents believed that children should mostly raise themselves. There were rules of course, but very little parental supervision as Mark's parents had numerous independent hobbies they enjoyed. During this time, Eric would terrorize Mark. Mark was meek, submissive, and only wanted everyone to get along. Eric on the other hand had an explosive temper as well as felt entitled to anything Mark had since he was the older brother.

One day Mark was sitting on the couch watching his favorite television show. Eric walked into the living room and abruptly snatched the remote out of Mark's hand and changed the channel to Sports. Without thinking Mark said "Hey! I was watching that!" Eric threw Mark off the couch and then pinned him to the floor. He punched Mark in the face and ribs over and over again. Mark couldn't even use his hands to cover his face because Eric had pinned Mark's arms down with his knees. As usual, there was nothing he could do to defend himself against Eric. Once Eric felt satisfied, he sat on the couch and watched TV as if nothing had happened. Mark remained crumpled on the floor for a few moments but then slinked off to his room. He got out a science fiction book to read but could barely see the print through his tears.

This was not the first time Eric had treated Mark like that. In fact, episodes like that one happened on a regular basis. Mark could not say "no" to Eric without receiving a vicious beat-down. In fact, Mark received so many bruises so frequently that one day at school he got called into the Principal's office. His teachers were concerned that Mark was possibly being abused at home. When Mark explained that it wasn't his parents who were beating him, but his brother. The school officials actually laughed, said a few jokes about "younger brothers", and then sent Mark back to class.

Mark's teachers were not the only ones to not take his abuse seriously. More than once Mark had cried to his parents "You never do anything!" Mark's parents would always give the same response "Just stay out of his way. You have to learn to stop annoying Eric. You know Eric has a temper. Brothers fight."

Mark's parents did not know how to handle conflict. Part of it was their naturally reserved personalities and the other part was that they were older parents and just didn't have the energy to deal with it. When Eric's parents tried to say "no" to him, he would fly off into a rage. He never hit his parents, but he would punch walls, break things, and say incredibly hurtful things to them. One such rage was due to Eric wanting $300 for a dirt bike. His parents didn't like the idea of their son having a potentially dangerous bike, nor did they have the money to spend frivolously. Although the family seemed to have all the comforts a family would want, in reality they had no savings and were living paycheck-to-paycheck.

They regretfully told Eric that they would have to say "no" to buying him a dirt bike. They just didn't have the money and what was he really going to do with a dirt bike anyways? His mother gingerly reminded him that most kids his age had after school jobs and if he saved his money he could buy one himself. Eric flew into a rage at the mention of him working. He screamed and yelled. He threw his arms into the air threateningly. One of his wild gestures caused a figurine to knock off a shelf and break. It had belonged to his mother's grandmother. Tears instantly flooded her face when she saw what had happened. "See what you made me do! If you had just given me the money like parents are supposed to do for their kids, this wouldn't have happened!" His mother pulled whatever money she had out of her purse and put it in his hand. Eric stormed off and slammed the door. Mark comforted his mother. As usual, Eric was never punished and the incident was never mentioned again.

Despite how awful Eric was to the entire family, everyone talked about him positively and seemed to admire him. No one ever talked about Mark or his achievements. Whenever Mark asked his parents about something, they'd answer "I bet your brother would know" or "You should ask your brother about that." It was like his brother was the authority on everything, and Mark just couldn't understand why.

When the brothers grew up, Mark stayed relatively close to his parents. He had a good job and a good marriage. Eric moved far away and had a slew of failed marriages. Eric voluntary cut himself off from the family, which hurt his parents very much. Eric seemed so angry at all of them, which Mark couldn't understand since Eric was always treated like a Prince. Several times Mark tried to have a relationship with Eric, only to have Eric become very angry at him for reasons Mark couldn't understand and then end contact once again.

Although Mark hadn't had much contact with Eric since adulthood, he still found himself thinking of Eric from time to time, mostly because the few times they did interact were so painful. He just could not understand why Eric seemed to hate him so much, or why his family seemed to think the abuse he suffered from Eric was "okay". How could Eric be so cruel to him?

It has only come to light relatively recently that a child can in fact be abused by a sibling, and that abuse, whether it is perpetrated by a parent or a sibling, is still abuse. The attitude until very recently was "Well, kids do fight". Another attitude was that "kids are innocent and incapable of abusing someone". Those of us who were bullied and abused as children know that kids are definitely capable of committing abuse and can be even scarier than adult abusers.

Sibling abuse is the most common form of family abuse (Button, Parker, & Gealt, 2008), and it is for that reason that it has earned its own chapter in this book. If you were abused by your parents, it is very likely that you were also abused by a sibling, if you had a sibling. And if you were abused by a sibling, it is very likely that no one took the matter seriously. One client described an incident at a family cook-out where her brother violently beat her and held a broken piece of glass to her throat. She genuinely believed that he was going to kill her. She desperately called out for help, but the adults just stayed seated in their chairs, watching what was happening, but not doing anything about it. No one cared. *That's just what siblings do, right?*

Like Mark, you probably found that when it came to defending yourself from your sibling, you were completely on your own. Your teachers and other authority figures saw the abuse as "a family matter", something to be dealt with by your family. Your parents saw it as just a matter of you and your sibling needing to learn to get along. You were probably told a million times "You need to learn to deal with this on your own". No one would ever say that to a child being abused by an adult, but they will freely say it to a child being abused by a sibling.

Learned helplessness

Perhaps more so than in any other kind of abuse, the message the abused child hears over and over again is that the abuse by their sibling is their fault. They are told "You need to learn to get along with your sister", "Your brother's just stressed, stop annoying him", "You need to stop bothering your siblings so much", "You need to try harder", and "Just suck it up".

In addition to no one stepping in to help the abused sibling or even seeing a problem with it, the child is helpless against their sibling. Often it is an older sibling that uses their size and strength to easily over-power the younger sibling. You have to remember that an older sibling is not just physically more advanced, but also mentally more advanced. Their brains are more developed and that allows them to be more cunning, more quick-witted, and more emotionally abusive with their words and actions.

Although the abuser is usually an older sibling, younger siblings being abusive is not unheard of. The younger sibling may get a free pass from parents because "they're the baby", while you are held to a higher standard because "you're old enough to know better." The younger sibling gets away with their abusive behavior while you get punished for fighting back. Sometimes younger siblings will gain up on the older sibling and take pleasure from the fact that they're younger but were still able to over-power someone older than them.

Whether the abusive sibling is older or younger, one thing that gives them an advantage is that they are often willing to take things to levels no sane person would be willing to go. Their reactions are over-blown and out of proportion. For instance, they may grab a knife during a fight or beat down your door if you run into your room for protection, or they may lock you out of the house for hours "just for fun". Their reaction is over-the-top and out of control.

Seemingly, once they get upset with you, things can escalate to such severe heights that as a child you may have even worried about your sibling one day killing you. Even if they wouldn't kill you, they would not feel any guilt about ruining your life, and that's very scary. One client's adult sibling became so angry with her that he used her name on the internet, posing as her, to make it look as though she was an admitted child molester. Now if an employer were to search for her name, dozens of pedophile websites came up with pro-molestation statements made under her name. My client wasn't even sure what she had done to make her brother so angry with her.

Because abusive siblings are so ruthless and so willing to take things to levels that normal people wouldn't go, the abused sibling feels helpless. Even if they are willing and able to fight back, the abusive sibling will just grab a knife or do something even worse. It's never a simple fight between siblings. Because of this, the abused sibling decides it's better to just tip toe around their abuser and try to placate them as much as possible. That's still never enough to avoid abuse, and when they do get abused they are told by adults that they were not placating enough and need to placate even more. The abused sibling cannot win.

When a person is in a situation like this, a natural result is to develop something recognized in psychology as "learned help-lessness". Learned helplessness is a big problem and is at the root of most of the common mental health disorders. Simply put, learned helplessness occurs when a person has been repeatedly subjected to painful experiences where they were helpless to stop the experience from happening. After a while, they just give up and expect and accept that painful experiences are going to happen to them no matter what. They don't do anything to change or avoid the situation even when they can. They simply accept their fate.

As a child, there was nothing you could do to stop the abuse from your sibling. It was your parent's job to protect you from that abuse but they did nothing. Now that you are an adult, you often have the ability to avoid or escape from abuse once it's started. However, you may find yourself putting up with it anyways. This is learned helplessness.

Learned helplessness sets you up for a lifetime of depression, anxiety, low self-esteem, and an inability to stand up for yourself or assert yourself. You've been almost desensitized to abuse and because of that you don't see the warning signs that other people see. You optimistically and gladly walk into relationships and situations that other people would avoid. Because of this, you end up in toxic work environments and abusive relationships.

Attitudes are changing, but sibling abuse is still widely regarded as just simple rivalry between siblings. Although your parents never took the abuse from your sibling seriously, and for the most part professionals don't take sibling abuse seriously either, it is very serious. It sets you up for a lifetime of abuse. And the worst part is that you accept the abuse as just being a part of life.

Why kids abuse other kids

Despite your sibling's abuse, you probably still loved them very much. You probably still do love them and would like to have a relationship with them. The sibling bond is very strong. It is then probably confusing to you how they could then be so cruel to you when you were a child; how they can still be so cruel to you now. *How can I love them so much despite how mean they have been to me? How can they hate me so much despite how kind I have been to them?*

Unfortunately, sibling abuse is not something that has been studied much in psychology. Again, it's really not something that has been taken seriously until relatively recently. However, I do think that psychology can shed some light on the situation. The important thing to remember is that there are many possible reasons for why your sibling acts the way they do. I'm going to discuss some of those reasons. These reasons may not be your sibling's reasons, but hopefully you will find something here that makes sense to you.

The first theory is that the sibling is modeling the abuse that they see taking place between their parents. I remember back when I worked with children, a mother brought in her seven year old son for therapy. She complained to me that his behavior was horrible. She said that if she didn't do what he wanted he would call her "a fucking bitch". Clearly this is strong language for a seven year old. You might expect this from a teenager, but it is highly unusual coming from a seven year old. I asked her who else in the family called her this. She tried to deny it at first, but then finally admitted that her live-in boyfriend frequently called her the same thing.

Back when I worked with children, I saw cases like that one constantly. Parents would bring their "problem child" into therapy and I would quickly learn that the child was simply imitating the things they observed from the adults in the family. Sometimes they would even be repeating things they heard from their parents word-for-word like in the previous example. Now, these children were brought into therapy because they were terrorizing their parents, but it doesn't take too much of a stretch of the imagination to assume that they were probably also terrorizing their siblings.

So these children see the way that their parents abuse each other or abuse them and they think "this is how things work in families". They may also see what's going on and sort of admire the abusive parent because everyone's scared of them or because the abuser seems to be "on the winning side". They want to be a winner too. They also learn that hitting or saying mean things is how you deal with anger, so they take out their frustration on their siblings as a way of letting off steam.

Modeling abusive behavior isn't the only reason why siblings abuse each other. We saw in the example of Mark and Eric that their parents were never abusive. To our knowledge, Eric was never abused by anyone. He was the favorite and was treated well by everyone in the family. So why was he so cruel to Mark? Another possible reason for sibling abuse is that the abuser is simply depressed.

Something that's important to remember is that adult depression can look very different from childhood depression. We all know what a depressed adult looks like: They are often lethargic, they sleep too much, they each too much, they cry a lot, they look sad all the time, they rarely leave the house if they don't have to, etc. Depressed kids can look like that too, but they can also look very different. Often times, depression in childhood manifests itself in acting-out behavior. This "acting-out behavior" can be violent and abusive in nature.

Instead of coming across as sad all the time, the depressed child seems very angry and easily frustrated. The child feels very sad on the inside, but the sadness comes out to other people as irritation. This is common for childhood depression. Unfortunately, sometimes it is misdiagnosed as bipolar disorder. If your sibling seemed angry all the time, they may have just been depressed. If this is the case, the depressed sibling probably regretted their actions and hated that they were so mean to you.

If the reason for your sibling's angry acting-out behavior was because they were depressed, then we would also expect them to eventually "grow out of it". With adulthood, the depression would either be alleviated or it would probably morph into the more typical looking adult depression. There's also the possibility that they would continue to have an agitated depression in adulthood, but this is rare.

Depression or some other mood disorder is a possible explanation, although in those cases we would expect that the sibling expresses lots of emotion but also lots of regrets after they flip out. What if they are like Mark's brother and don't seem to feel any regret? What if they are callous and calculating in the abuse they commit?

In Graduate School I elected to take a criminal psychology class. Criminal psychology involves interesting things like FBI profiling but also theories as to why people behave in a criminal manner or hurt other people. When I took the class, I was expecting to hear the professor say that people become criminals because they suffered through poverty, they experienced great adversity, or they grew up in a dysfunctional household. Those things certainly may play a part in why people turn to petty crime (Eitle, 2010), but it was not the reason why people go on to be the type of criminal that intentionally hurts other people (Wikstrom, 2004).

If you were abused by your sibling, your sibling intentionally hurt you. Abuse is intentional in nature. If they had done to a stranger what they had done to you, they would most likely be put in jail. The odds are likely that your abusive sibling has committed other crimes in addition to what they have done to you. Perhaps they have already served some jail time for other crimes they have committed. For that reason, I think that criminal psychology may be appropriate for providing us with an explanation for why your sibling was so cruel to you.

What I learned in Criminal Psychology shocked me. Although the popular held belief is that people commit violent crime because they were good people who suffered adversity and were led astray at some point in their young lives, the actual science doesn't show that at all. Study after study after study reveals that they are very different from the rest of us and they seem to just be born this way (Samenow, 2012).

What makes them different from the rest of us? To begin with, they don't feel remorse for the bad things they do and they don't feel empathy for the suffering of other people (Herpertz & Sass, 2000). In other words, when they hurt other people, they don't feel bad about it. In fact, they often enjoy it. Remember how I said that there are people in society that exploit other people? Well, all of those people were at some point children and most had siblings. Sometimes we're unfortunate enough to have one of these people as a brother or sister.

In psychology, we use the terms narcissist, psychopath, and sociopath for the most part interchangeably. That is because they all have the same thing in common: They don't feel empathy for other people and they don't feel remorse for the bad things they do. They feel totally justified in their behavior, *always*. It is also widely believed that they are unable to feel love for another person. When they do feel a liking for another person, it is because they feel able to dominate or exploit that person (Campbell, Foster, & Finkel, 2002). This is why your sibling was able to repeatedly be so cruel to you while you continuously sought to have a relationship with them.

Lay people commonly refer to this as the "bad seed" theory and it's relatively hard for people to accept the concept of it. We don't like to think that there is such a thing as "bad people" and we especially don't like to think that they could exist in our own families. This idea that good people can be pushed to do bad things is much more palatable. One of the major reasons why it exists is because predators naturally use this excuse in order to gain sympathy from other people and perhaps leniency and parole. They say they only do bad things because they had bad things happen to them, and we believe them because we want to believe that they are really good people on the inside and have an ability to reform.

One of the most common myths in regards to criminal behavior has to do with sex offenders specifically. The myth is that people who are sex offenders do what they do because at some point, someone raped or molested them. This is often referred to as the "vampire theory" or "vampirism". In lore, someone becomes a vampire because they were bitten by a vampire. So the theory goes that someone becomes a sex offender because they were once the victim of a sex offender themselves.

I actually used to work at a sex offender treatment facility. And sure enough, all of the guys there claimed to have been molested as children and abused. Usually they claimed to have been abused by their very own parents. I think the other therapists there liked to believe this because it made them feel better about the work they were doing. People like this theory, but is it accurate or are the offenders just trying to manipulate us?

Before I talk about the actual science, let's just take a moment to use common sense. If it's true that being sexually assaulted causes you to become a sex offender, wouldn't we expect most offenders to be women? After all, women make up the majority of victims, and yet, female sex offenders are very rare (Bader, et all, 2010). You would also expect there to be way more sex offenders than their actually are. Let's just look at men for this, since someone might argue there are gender differences that might explain why "vampirism" works for male offenders but not women. 1 in 6 men have been sexually abused, about 1 in 20 men will go on to commit sexual abuse at some point in their lives. If vampirism is true, then why don't the numbers add up?

If we're able to dispel this myth very easily just by using common sense, then why is it so popular? Again, people like the vampirism theory because it makes the offender more sympathetic. Early studies also seemed to support this theory at first and therapists happily jumped on the band wagon. The problem with these early studies is that they were relying on the offender's self-report for data. The researcher would ask the offender if they had been abused themselves and they would of course say "yes", just as they all had at the facility that I had been working at. It wasn't until someone decided to actually give them a lie-detector test that we were able to find out the truth. As it turns out, only 30% of sex offenders were ever sexually abused themselves (Becker & Murphy, 1998). This 30% figure is in line with the percentage of the general public that was also sexually abused at some point in their lives. Sex offenders are no more likely to have been abused than anybody else.

Why am I focusing so much on sex offenders in particular? Because when I worked at that sex offender treatment facility, I noticed a pattern with the offenders. They didn't just jump into raping and molesting strangers, almost all of them had started at home. There seemed to be a pattern where they would first start abusing the family pets. After that they moved on to their younger siblings. Many of the clients from dysfunctional families I have worked with have been sexually abused by a sibling and have a lot of questions regarding why their sibling would do that to them.

Sex offenders offend against their siblings for the most part because they can. They're in the same home with you, you trust them, and they predict that it's unlikely that you will tell on them. Even if you do tell, they may predict that it's very unlikely that their parents would believe you or really do anything about it. When you take someone who is born without the ability to feel remorse or empathy plus a home with little parental supervision, you get an environment where siblings can abuse other siblings.

But is it really possible that a sociopath could be born into a loving family? It does happen. Consider the case of Jeffrey Dahmer. Jeffrey Dahmer, perhaps the most infamous sociopath and serial killer was raised in a loving middle class family. He grew up in a nice home in the suburbs where both parents were present. And yet, from an early age he took pleasure in dismembering animals. His younger brother David went on to live a perfectly normal life. Jeffrey was an anomaly.

After reading all of this, you may suspect other family members of being sociopaths or narcissists too. But how does one know if their sibling was a sociopath or just depressed or just acting out what they witnessed from their parents?

Narcissists

The truth is, you may never know the reason why your sibling or parent abused you. Narcissism and sociopathy are very hard to diagnose, even for the experienced therapist. Narcissists typically have very low insight and feel right in every instance. They hide or minimize incidents of them wronging others, and for the most part therapists only know what their clients tell them. The therapist often has to work with the client for a while before they have a hint that the person is narcissistic or antisocial.

No one knows what really goes on in another person's head. There's really no way to tell if someone really feels remorse or is just faking it or vice versa. Not all narcissists are violent or sex offenders. In fact, most are not. Although they are prone to rage, most are merely self-absorbed, attention-seeking, and unable to relate to other people. It has also proved difficult to determine just what percentage of the population is narcissistic. Seemingly every study comes up with a different figure and it seems to vary depending on which country the study took place.

According to the Continuum of Self Theory (Rosenberg, 2013), we all have narcissistic traits, it's just a matter of degree, with only a small percentage actually meeting the full criteria for being a narcissist. Again, we don't know what percentage of the population actually meet the criteria for narcissism, but most likely it is less than 10%. The percentage that is violent, is even less than that.

Although offenders don't create other offenders, there is reason to believe that narcissists may create other narcissists. There is a lot of evidence that narcissism is at least in part genetic or biological (Lou, et all, 2014). And where do we get our genetics from? *Our parents.* Although narcissistic parents don't always breed narcissistic children, narcissistic children almost always have an identifiable narcissistic parent. Typically in a family where there is one narcissist, there are often several. It has also been said that in every dysfunctional family there is at least one narcissist.

In order to understand your sibling, and perhaps even your dysfunctional family as a whole, you need to have an understanding of narcissism. As stated previously, we all have narcissistic traits to some degree, with some people being hardly narcissistic at all and other people being rather narcissistic. As far as a person actually being diagnosed as narcissistic by a mental health professional, the diagnosis would actually fall into one of the four Cluster B Personality Disorders. They are: Narcissistic Personality Disorder, Antisocial Personality Disorder, Histrionic Personality Disorder, and Borderline Personality Disorder.

These Cluster B personality disorders are where narcissism comes to its extreme. I would warn you though against trying to diagnose your family yourself. It's really something that should only be done by a qualified mental health professional. If you have strong suspicions that a sibling or family member is a narcissist, it would be helpful to talk about that with a therapist. The therapist can help you to better understand if they are or are not a narcissist and strategies you can use to avoid further harm from them.

That being said, narcissists are characterized by an extreme self-absorption. Other people's needs don't exist in their minds. It's all about them and they are always right. They feel that they are better than other people. They are more brilliant or more important than other people. They often consider themselves to be intellectuals, even if they don't really know what they are talking about. They often have a "the rules don't apply to me" attitude, and because of that they are often extreme hypocrites. They believe they are special and know how to "cheat the system". This belief is then applied to criminal behavior, gambling, drug use, and infidelity.

Narcissists also dominate conversations and become annoyed when someone or something shifts the attention from them. When they do nice things for other people, it's in order to manipulate people or try to earn back a favor later. They are much more selfish than the average person. It's all about them. Disappearances are not uncommon. It's not unusual for a narcissist to just "take off" one day without warning. If presented with evidence that they are not in fact better than other people, the narcissist goes off into what is referred to as a "narcissistic rage". Their interactions with other people commonly involve manipulation and "playing games".

There is significance in why psychologists refer to narcissism as a "personality disorder". A person's personality is for the most part something that they are born with (Dweck, 2007). This is what makes a personality disorder so difficult to treat. By its very definition, it is pervasive, chronic, and resistant to change. If your relative is a narcissist or has a personality disorder, it is very unlikely that they will ever change and this is something that you will have to accept about them.

Entire books have been written about narcissism, and I could certainly write chapters on it myself. However, I fear that that would take away from the focus on my book. That being said, if you wish to understand more about narcissism, I highly recommend the excellent book "The Sociopath Next Door" by Martha Stout.

Even if your sibling is not a narcissist but rather is simply depressed or merely picked up bad habits from watching your parents, you still have to accept that you do not have the power to change them. They will only change if they want to change and you cannot convince them that they want to change. They have to find that within themselves. Despite what your family may want you to believe, you are also not responsible for their behavior.

The sibling void

Just like how in the last chapter I wrote that "your parent is still your parent", your sibling is still your sibling. You love them for the simple fact that they are your sibling. It's hard to imagine loving someone who has treated you worse than your worst enemy, and yet people continue to love their abusive sibling. Despite the horrible things that you have been subjected to, you probably would still prefer to have a relationship with your sibling if you could.

We can't help but love our siblings. When we were little, we desperately wanted them to love us back. We wanted to feel "included". We wanted to make them feel proud of us. We wanted to impress them. We wanted to be accepted. We wanted to be special to them. We just wanted to be loved. But instead of loving us, they repeated hurt us and rejected us.

Even as an adult, you probably still are trying to be loved by your sibling. You're still asking yourself "Why aren't I good enough?" This is the void that our sibling leaves. It's a place in our soul where sibling love should have been. Even if we resolve that we simply cannot have a relationship with our sibling because of their abuse, it is likely that the void will always remain.

Conclusion

Up until recently, sibling abuse was not something that was taken seriously. To an extent, it still isn't. Parents still dismiss it as simple sibling rivalry and it's usually not until something extreme happens that they realize it's more serious. Although I have found in my career that parental denial can be a powerful thing.

If you were abused by your sibling, and possibly are still being mistreated, then you know that sibling aggression and sibling abuse is very real. You know the damaging effect it has had on you.

You know how it has left you wondering "Is it just me? Am I really this horrible? Why would my sister treat me this way?"

There are a number of reasons why your sibling did what they did, and none of them are your fault. Yes, siblings annoy each other from time to time, but there are better ways your sibling could have dealt with that. Abuse is always wrong and your parent should have done more to protect you and ensure that you two got along.

Your sibling did what they did, not because of you, but because of them. There are a lot of different possible explanations for why they acted the way they did. One possibility is that they learned their hurtful behaviors from watching your parents interact. Another possibility is that they had untreated mental illness. Again, this is something that your parent should have picked up on and taken your sibling to get help. If they tried to get help and it wasn't effective, they should have kept trying until they found something that worked. If that's the case, then your sibling was just as much a victim of neglect as you were.

Lastly, your sibling may have mistreated you because they were a narcissist. We know that narcissists exist in our society and at some point in their lives they were children and had siblings that they terrorized. That sibling may have been you. If they are a narcissist, then most likely they continue to terrorize you even though you are both adults. If you suspect that this may be the case, then I strongly recommend that you contact a therapist. A therapist can help you sort out the hurt and confusing feelings that result from having a narcissist in your family.

Part 2

Taking your power back

4

Taking yourself out of the equation

Melody was an only child. She didn't know much about her father, just that he was much older than her mother and that her mother had become pregnant with her at 19. Her father married her mother and they lived together in his house in California. One day when Melody was only 2, her mother packed up the car and took her to Massachusetts. Once in Boston, she divorced Melody's father and Melody never saw him again. She doesn't remember her "great escape" to Massachusetts, and only knows what her mother would tell her about it. The few times she spoke to her father on the phone and asked him about it, he would say in a sad voice "We just didn't get along" and that was it.

Melody's grandfather was also much older than his wife and was somewhat well-off. Not fabulously wealthy, but when he died Melody's mother got a comfortable inheritance. She then used this money to buy a small but nice house and support herself. Although at one point the inheritance had been a hefty sum, there wasn't much left now as Melody's mom had foolishly invested it in failed venture after failed venture. When Melody was 8, her mother bought a hair salon and decided that she was qualified to cut hair. She hired a few other stylists but she could never keep an employee for long. Eventually she just closed the salon at a loss.

Then Melody's mother decided that she wanted to be a horse broker. A horse broker is essentially someone who just buys and resells horses. Her mother didn't have any expertise when it came to horses but felt qualified none-the-less. No surprise, this ended up being another failed venture. There was a series of failed businesses while Melody was growing up. Her mother's latest thing was a pet-sitting service. At least this one wasn't financially risky, but it wasn't really bringing in any money either. Melody worried constantly about what would happen when her mother ran out of her grandfather's inheritance. She worried that it was almost gone now.

Growing up, Melody's mother was constantly stressed about these businesses. Despite her initial confidence, she would quickly learn that she didn't know how to run a business. Rather than accept that about herself and move on, she would blame Melody. She blamed Melody for being "too needy", "too time-consuming", and "a brat". She would repeatedly tell Melody that if she had never been born that she would be a successful business woman by now.

Melody always tried her best to please her mother but it was never good enough. It seemed that no matter what she did it was always her fault and her mother would scream and rage and say horrible things to her. If she got especially worked up she would destroy Melody's things. A few times she had beat Melody with a shoe or plastic hanger. Her mother would scream at Melody to move out of the house and threaten to kick her out at least a couple times per week. No matter what happened, Melody's step-dad would always take her mother's side and tell Melody that she needed to be a better daughter.

When Melody's mother would go off on these rages, which were frequent, it was truly scary for Melody. She didn't know how to describe it other than just that her mother became "a monster". The few times she had told other people about her mother's behavior, no one believed her. Melody's mother seemed great to everyone else and always knew what to say to come across like the perfect mother.

At 25 years old, Melody was in graduate school working towards her MBA. She had never lived outside her mother's home and had never had a job. The times she had talked about getting a job her mother would say "It doesn't make sense to get a job. After you graduate we're going to open a business together. If you got a job, you'd just get yourself fired." Other excuses were "But how would you get to work? You don't have a car! The car would cost more than you'd make at the job so it doesn't make any sense to get a job."

Melody was completely dependent on her mother, and her mother used that to her advantage. She would repeatedly shut off Melody's phone or take away her computer if Melody dared to express any independence. She complained bitterly how Melody didn't contribute any money to the house and was such a burden.

To Melody it seemed that her mother desperately wanted her out of the house. Ever the people-pleaser, Melody set off to find a job and an apartment. She was actually able to find a job within walking distance of her school. One of her classmates was looking for a new roommate and the rent was affordable. She could move in next month. When Melody told her mother about her plans, she was expecting her mother to be over-joyed. Maybe now she would finally be proud of her. Instead she was enraged. Melody's mother shifted back and forth between being angry and crying hysterically. She called Melody every name in the book, and then she begged her to stay.

Not knowing what to do, Melody ran out of the house. She couldn't believe what was happening. Wasn't this what her mother had always wanted, to get rid of her? It didn't make sense for her mom to be angry about her leaving. It was then that she realized that it wasn't her. There was nothing wrong with her, it was her mother. Her mother was the one with problems, not her. It was like suddenly realizing that everything she had ever believed was a lie. Suddenly, a fog had been lifted over her entire life.

Hopefully, like Melody, you're starting to see the truth when it comes to your dysfunctional family. You understand now that no matter how much they try to convince you that it's your fault, it really isn't. Maybe you're not fully convinced yet, but we'll talk more about that later. For now, I'm happy that you're just starting to see that you are merely a piece in a larger puzzle that is your family.

You've been put into a role that's part of an equation that works for your parent or whoever the narcissist is in your family. The equation is meant to give them the most benefit. Odds are likely that like Melody, you don't get any benefit from this equation and would like to take yourself out of it. In the next few chapters I'm going to give you directions on how to do judt that. The first step is removing your family's leverage over you.

In functional families, there is no leverage. Relationships are built on respect, not dominance and the threat of abandonment. In that sense, dysfunctional families are very much like a cult. Have you ever wondered what the difference was between a cult and just a regular church or spiritual group? In a cult, the leader has complete control. They exercise leverage in order to keep this control. This leverage may be that they have control over your money or that they will turn your family against you if you question the leader's authority. There is also a direct or implied threat that they will make your life miserable if you try to leave the cult. Dysfunctional families use much of the same tactics.

If you truly want to take yourself out of the equation and take your life back, the first step is to remove the leverage that your family has over you. This often includes a mix of financial leverage and emotional leverage.

Financial leverage

It is very common in dysfunctional families for the parent or narcissist to try to keep the person financially tied to them for as long as possible. In normal families, children are encouraged to get a part-time job when they are in High School and the parents slowly start shifting financial responsibility to their child. Of course, along the way they teach them things like how to keep track of their spending, how to responsibly use a credit card, and how to do their taxes. In dysfunctional families the parent never uses these teaching moments and the kid is either on their own or "not allowed" to do their own finances.

I have had many a client in their 20's who had no clue as to how to do their taxes, open their own bank account, write a check, nothing, because their parent insisted they were not responsible enough to learn how to do these things. In functional families, parents are thrilled when their adult child starts paying their own bills. In dysfunctional families, it is seen as a threat.

One of the biggest problems is that the parent is very good at convincing their adult child that it's better that way. *It makes sense* to stay on your parent's car insurance. *It makes sense* to live with them while you save up for a house. *It makes sense* to be on a "family plan" for your phone. And of course, they want to make it seem like you're the one getting the most out of the deal. After all, you're the one getting free car insurance, etc.

But I want you to take a moment to think about it. Are you really the one benefitting here? Or is it your parents? When you allow them to financially support you, even if it's only partial support, you are giving them leverage over you. By living with them, you are under their rule and watchful eye. They can make demands on you and feel entitled to making your decisions for you because you're living in their house. They can also threaten to kick you out if you try to stand up for yourself.

Even if you're living on your own, if they are still paying any of your bills or giving you a monthly amount of money, they have leverage. Because you're on their car insurance, they feel entitled to tell you how and when you drive your own car. By being on their cell phone plan, they can now look at the phone numbers you call. It's just another way for them to continue to exert some kind of control over you and violate your privacy.

If you try to take yourself out of the equation while you are still dependent on them financially, they now have the ability to threaten your livelihood. Or even if they don't threaten you, at the very least they won't take you seriously because in their minds you are still a child who can't handle adult responsibilities.

There are two different ways of looking at adulthood. One way of looking at it is that you become an adult when you turn 18 or 21. Another way of determining adulthood is when a person achieves certain milestones. These milestones often include having a full-time job, living outside the family home, and not taking any money what-so-ever from your parents. You probably look at adulthood in terms of age while your parent looks at it in terms of these milestones.

By not being an independent and self-sufficient adult, you are really just an adolescent to your parent. Don't believe me? Let's take a look at the case of Bill. Bill was a client of mine that came to therapy because he was having problems with his narcissistic father. Bill was 36 years old. Bill made hand-made wooden furniture that was both sculptural and functional. They were truly beautiful pieces, but it's hard to support yourself as an artist. Sometimes sales were good and sometimes they weren't. He had originally wanted to get a teaching degree so he could have a steady paycheck while making furniture on the side. This certainly would have been a wise and prudent decision, but Bill's father always discouraged him from going to college.

Bill's father constantly told him that he wasn't cut-out for college and that he would just flunk out or waste his money if he went. Besides, teachers supposedly don't make any money. At the same time he was constantly criticized Bill for not taking initiative or following through with his dreams. The truth was, being an art teacher at a High School or Community College wasn't good enough for Bill's father. He had dreams of his son being a famous artist and wouldn't accept less than that. It infuriated Bill that his father seemed to believe that selling this furniture should be as easy as walking down the street and that the only reason why Bill wasn't famous yet was because Bill was lazy.

Bill didn't live with his father, thankfully. He lived in a modest apartment and relied on public transportation to get place to place. He used to have a roommate but his father convinced him to get rid of the roommate. His father thought it was "beneath him" to have a roommate to help with expenses. Another financial problem was that Bill's life was so miserable and joyless because of his father, the only way he knew how to get any pleasure out of his life was to go out several times a week. He went to restaurants and bars with other artist-types. He drank expensive wine. He tried to impress women. He wanted to give off the image of a successful artist and entrepreneur. It was the only time he felt good about himself, and he relied on his father to subsidize his lifestyle. After all, the "real him" wasn't good enough.

Bill knew he was living a lie. He knew that what he was doing was unsustainable and couldn't go on forever. He knew that anyone who got close to him would learn the truth and then he would feel ashamed of himself. The good news is that after a few sessions with Bill, he was starting to take his life back and take himself out of the equation. But how do I know that Bill's father thought of him as just an adolescent?

Well, one day I received a mysterious email. I didn't recognize the email address and it wasn't really clear who it was from. It definitely wasn't from any of my clients. The email was very long but I took the time to read it. From reading the email, you would swear to God that it was a father writing about his 16 year old son. Years ago I used to work with a lot of "out of control teens" (Hint: Most of them are just normal kids in dysfunctional families), but it had been a while since I had had a teenage client. So I just wrote back "Sorry, I think you may have emailed the wrong therapist" and never got another response.

When Bill came in for his next appointment he told me that his father found out that he was seeing me and may have sent me an email to "set the record straight". Bill then confirmed his father's email address and I realized that it had been him. His son was 36 years old, well past the age where most men are living their own lives and have their own families, but his father still viewed him as he would a 16 year old and treated him as such.

When your parents have financial leverage over you, it makes them feel that not only can they control you and influence your decisions, but they still very much see you as a child. If you truly want this behavior to stop, the first thing you need to do is to remove the leverage. Now, I'm not expecting you to do all of this overnight, but I do expect you to at least start taking steps towards independence.

The first thing you need to do is to start paring down on your expenses. Minimize them as much as you possibly can. There are people in this country who are able to live completely independent of their parents even though they have no money. If you are truly impoverished, there are government services that can help you. The help is out there, you just need to ask for it.

I know what it's like to be just starting out on your own and struggling. When I was getting my Masters, I was a full-time student, I worked a full-time job, and I was doing my internship full-time. How did I do it? Well, two nights a week I would go without sleep so I had the time to get my school work done. In other words, I did what I had to do. However, I also felt really proud of myself. I did it all on my own and that feels good. I paid for my own education, my own car, etc.

Later on when I decided to go into private practice, I knew it was going to be difficult for the first couple of years. I would be giving up benefits and a steady income, and there was a lot of risk. To minimize that risk, I started paring down. I stopped spending money unless it was absolutely necessary. I got rid of any expense I could, including cable. I even sold my car. This allowed me to step out on my own without worrying about how I was going to be able to pay my bills.

After I got rid of all of the luxuries in my life, I realized how meaningless they were. We spend so long thinking that "things" will make us happy, and then when those "things" go away, you realize that they never really had an impact on your life. You realize that it's better to be independent and feel good about the life you live than have a bunch of stuff.

The narcissist wants you to think that you can't survive without them; that you need "things" in your life in order to feel good about yourself, but you don't. You CAN survive on your own. Unlike the narcissist, you can live below your means. You don't need to put up a false front to feel good about yourself. And believe me, you will feel good about yourself once you become an independent and self-sufficient adult.

Emotional leverage

Financial leverage is not the only leverage that your family uses in order to control you. The other tool is emotional leverage. Let me be clear that when I say that you also need to remove their emotional leverage that I am not at all implying that you stop loving them or somehow stop feeling things when it comes to your family. Your feelings are valid and you have a right to them. The goal is not to get you to stop loving your family.

Emotional leverage is when you use someone else's emotions in order to manipulate them. There's a reason why narcissists are often called "emotional manipulators". We trust them with our emotions and then they later use those same emotions against us as weapons.

It's important to understand that we will not be able to get rid of all of the emotional leverage our family has. Because they are family, rather than just strangers, they will always have some amount of emotional leverage over us. Because we will always love them to some degree, they will always have emotional leverage. We will never be able to get rid of it completely, but we can minimize it. We can minimize it in two ways: By no longer inviting the emotional manipulator to celebrate our successes nor mourn our losses.

One of the key aspects of being in a dysfunctional family is that we are conditioned to feel that we *need* their approval in order to feel good about ourselves. We cannot celebrate our successes without their reassurance that it is indeed a success. We feel that we cannot mourn a loss unless they give us permission to mourn it. Because we were never taught how to, or given the encouragement to regulate our own emotions, we rely on our family to do it for us. This gives them incredible emotional leverage over us. This gives them a lot of power over us.

It's natural to want to celebrate your successes and mourn your losses with your family. This is normal. When we succeed we are hoping to get a pat on the back to make the success feel that much better. When we lose, we are looking for sympathy and encouragement to help us not feel so bad about it. I want you to pause and take a moment to think about this. Does your family really provide you with this? If they do, great! You can skip this section. If they don't, keep reading.

We often find in dysfunctional families that our family, or at least certain family members, celebrate our losses and mourn our successes. They seem to take pleasure in us failing. They spread the juicy gossip of our loss to other family members and gush about it. They take pleasure in lording it over us. They scold us or give a self-satisfied "I told you so". Instead of feeling better, we leave feeling worse. Instead of feeling encouraged, we feel defeated. Another common way of responding to our losses is that they may minimize it. For example, "This isn't a loss. Get over it. God, you're melodramatic". This minimization makes us feel ever worse because not only have we suffered a loss, but apparently we're also weak and pathetic. It becomes a double-blow.

Sharing your successes with your family can be just as upsetting. There's a few different ways that they tend to react to successes that ruins it for you:

1. "I still expect better". Instead of being happy for you, they show you how it's not really an achievement. For example, let's say you landed your first job as a full-time teacher. Instead of being happy for you, they tell you that the school you will be working for has a bad reputation or how some other school would have been better.
2. "Meh". In this case, your family member responds to your good news with disinterest. They give the impression "why would you bother telling me this?" Or they give a quick "Congratulations!" and then quickly change the subject back to them.

3. "Stop bragging!" Your family member accuses you of bragging or sharing your success with the intention of making them feel bad about themselves. They accuse you of rubbing it in their faces. All three of these reactions steal your thunder and leaving you feeling depressed about your own achievement.

So why is it considered emotional leverage to respond to your successes and losses in this manner? Because it allows them to have control over the way you feel about the things that happen to you. They rob you of the joy of your achievements and make losses feel that much worse. There's never any relief. The driving message is "You're incompetent". Once it gets to the point that you've internalized this message and believe it, they now will have a great deal of control over you.

Your family knows that people have a natural tendency to share news of successes or losses with their family first, usually mom and dad. By responding to both in such a negative way, it then makes you not want to share the news with anyone else afterwards. You feel embarrassed and keep it to yourself or minimize it if you do tell it to anyone else. After a while this creates a pattern where you are only going to your family or one family member in particular, for emotional support. This thus increases the amount of control and leverage that person has over you. Control and leverage is everything to them and it's primarily why they do what they do.

When I explain all of this to my clients, a common response is "What's the point of all of this then if I can't share my successes and losses with my family?" My response to this is "What's the point of sharing your successes and losses with your family if they only make you feel worse afterwards?" I'm not saying that you have to be a hermit from now on. Rather, I'm suggesting that you instead share this information with people who are actually supportive. This may mean telling some family members, but not others. This may mean not telling any family members about the ups and downs in your life.

Although many of my clients are skeptical of this at first, the ones who actually follow through report feeling much better later. There is an initial sadness that comes with realizing that your family is unsupportive, but it is then followed by a sense of relief once you're able to get that support from other people. Things that were missing from your life start to come back into it. Things like: Joy, excitement, pride, satisfaction, comfort, connection, etc. Once you're able to get that support again, most people report feeling stronger every day.

There is another type of emotional leverage that dysfunctional family members often resort to that's slightly different from the one previously described. It's called emotional extortion. Emotional extortion is when the person gets your trust by seeming supportive at the time. They're so good at making you feel at ease, that you tell them things that you can't believe you told them; perhaps even things that you have never told anyone before.

The most common example of this is when you end up telling the person too much information about your romantic relationship or marriage. In particular, you end up giving them information that makes your spouse look bad. I've often wondered if the reason why the spouse is so often targeted is because the family views them as being their biggest competition.

Once they have gotten this information from you, they hold on to it and then use it against you later. In terms of a spouse, they may use the information you gave them to try to break up your marriage or at the very least start conflicts in your relationship. Even if they don't do this, just the threat of it gives them leverage. It makes you hesitate to stand up for yourself knowing that they have so much leverage on you. Don't give them that power.

So you might be wondering what to do if you've already told them too much and given them a lot of leverage. The good news is that the currency of information decreases in value with each passing year. Eventually so much time has passed that even if they threaten to reveal your secrets, who cares? Eventually these things have happened so long ago that no one cares anymore. The best thing to do is to still just stop giving them information now.

How much information is too much? Only you can really determine that. Don't ever give them anything that can be used against you, especially if it's the same type of information that they have used against you in the past. It may take some trial and error, but eventually you will figure out how much and what type of information you can give.

As a general rule, you should avoid complaining about other people to or in front of the narcissist. This is the type of information they love getting because it is often the most useful when it comes to manipulating or sabotaging you socially. I want you to especially avoid saying anything about your significant other that could be interpreted as being negative. In general it's a good policy to only say positive things about your partner to other people. If you're in the process of breaking up with someone, that's a whole other issue. If you want to make it work with your partner or are trying to preserve the relationship, then save your complaints for a therapist or couples counselor. You will thank me for this later.

Another type of emotional leverage is emotional hijacking. In emotional hijacking, the person essentially hijacks your feelings. They figure out what your sensitivities are and then say or do certain things to cause you to feel (and hopefully act) in a certain way. They then use your feelings to coerce you into doing something that's to their advantage.

Probably the most common example of this is when parents use guilt to get their adult children to spend inordinate amounts of time with them, call them all the time, move back to their home town, give their parents money, etc. I've talked a lot about you using your family for financial and emotional support, but I recognize that it goes the other way around too. There are plenty of people in dysfunctional families where the family uses the person's feelings of guilt and obligation in order to exploit them.

In cases of emotional hijacking, you frequently feel drained and exhausted by the person. Just like in the case of a car hijacking, they've used up all of your fuel and are still demanding more! You can feel like you are helpless to stop it. The times you've tried to say "no" just resulted in emotional anguish. You feel like the bad guy and they've convinced you that you are just one favor away from being their hero. It's an emotional rollercoaster.

Emotional hijacking is extremely passive aggressive. It allows the person to aggress against you but at the same time allows them to passively deny any aggression if confronted by you. That's one of the things that are so troubling about it. It can be hard for the person to tell if their being emotionally hijacked or if the person's just genuinely desperate.

Most of the clients that I've had where their family uses emotional hijacking have genuinely believed that their family just does this because they truly have nowhere to turn. However, if you really think it through, they have tons of options other than you. Options like government assistant, professional help, their own spouse, or an old friend. When you think about it, those options make more sense and are actually better. But is it manipulation or does the person simply not realize there are better options?

I can't tell you if you're being manipulated or not. I've never met your family and I don't know your exact situation. But consider this old adage: If it looks like a duck, walks like a duck, and quacks like a duck, it's probably a duck. If it looks like manipulation, it probably is.

Your next question probably is: Okay, so how do I stop it? Whether it's manipulation or not, the strategy is still the same: When your family member tries to guilt you into doing something, all you have to do is turn it around on them. When they are using their "sad feelings" to try to coerce you, so all you do is do the same. Just say something like "Mom, when you say that (put me in this position, say I don't visit enough even though I see you several times a year, etc) it makes me feel really bad." If they try to explain themselves, just keep repeating "It makes me feel bad when you say things like that."

If they are not trying to manipulate you, they'll realize that they are unfairly burdening you and stop. If they are trying to manipulate you, they'll realize that this tactic no longer works on you and will stop. Either way it stops, so that's the good news. The bad news is that it may take a few tries before they get it. Just keep following through and eventually they will stop.

Now in case you feel guilty doing this, it's good to know that you really have nothing to feel guilty about. Let me explain why: Once you stop enabling your family member, they will naturally turn to those better options for support. And because of that, they'll end up getting better care and assistance than they were getting before. In that sense, you're actually helping them much more by not helping them! Also, let's not forget that unless the person is much younger than you that there was a time when they got along fine without you. In situations where the person really can't help themselves because they are young, elderly, or medically in danger, you are still better off making a phone call to the appropriate professional help than trying to do everything by yourself.

Getting your power back

You may understand why it's philosophically a good idea to remove all of your dysfunctional family's leverage over you, but fail to see how it will actually change anything. You might be wondering if it's really to your benefit to say no to free money or stop sharing certain things with them. You may doubt your family would even care that you're making these sacrifices.

As I had mentioned previously, this is a process. You're going to need to first build a foundation before you can take your life back. I wish all of this was easier, I really do. In fact, I'm always researching and trying to find ways of making things easier. Unfortunately, it is not as easy as just visualizing your family treating you better. If it was that easy, there would be no dysfunctional families left in the world. The only way to succeed is to be stubborn, even more stubborn than your family.

Removing your family's leverage over you is the first step. This is what builds that foundation and it is absolutely essential to change. Does this mean that you have to be absolutely 100%

independent before moving on with the rest of the steps in this book? No. But you do need to at least *start* removing leverage. Removing all of your family's leverage is going to take time. There are few people reading this book that are in a position where by tomorrow they will have completely freed themselves. But I do expect that by tomorrow you will have at least started to make moves towards more emotional and financial freedom. Baby-steps are fine. If anything, as a therapist I have found that people who make baby-steps are often better at maintaining progress in the long term than those that hastily make a large leap.

While you are making these baby-steps, you can start implementing the other steps that are recommended in this book. You can do both at once, although I think that you will find that the other things will be easier to accomplish once you have decreased a good amount of the leverage your family has over you. Once you have removed all of the leverage, you will be surprised just how easy and effective the other tasks in this book become.

Why is removing leverage so important? Functional families are based on mutual respect. In dysfunctional families, there is often very little respect or a situation where certain family members demand a high level of respect while rarely if ever reciprocating. What we find in toxic families is a system of dysfunction built on power and control. Where does power and control come from? It comes from the amount of leverage you have over other people.

When you remove the leverage they have over you, you get your power back. Once you have your power back, you can start changing the way your family treats you. Let me just remind you that the goal here isn't to flip things around so that you now have power over your family or certain family members. You have probably seen other family members try to accomplish this and all it did was backfire on them or simply help to maintain the dysfunction. It's not about over-powering them, out-smarting them, or "winning". The only way to win is to not play the game.

And that's what we are doing. We are taking ourselves out of the game. It's not about trying to change the equation so that we can come out on top. It's about taking yourself out of the equation completely so that you are free to choose your own life.

When you take your power back, you will notice a difference almost immediately. Of course you will feel good about yourself, but probably even better than you would have thought. When I first became financially independent from my family, I knew it was the right thing to do but I didn't really expect I'd feel good about it. If anything, I expected I would feel more stressed out! I was surprised how good I felt. I was perhaps always a bit more financially independent than my peers. Even as a child I didn't like taking money away from my parents and got a job as soon as I was old enough to. I had bought my own car, my own car insurance, and paid for my own schooling, both undergrad and graduate school, but when the day came where I no longer had any financial ties to my parents and hadn't taken a single dime from them in years, it felt incredible. I felt so proud of myself. It meant that I could take full credit for my own accomplishments. It also removed a lot of my fears and anxieties because now I knew myself to be a capable person.

I want you to be able to have that same feeling for yourself. It's incredibly freeing and I think it's something that everyone wants. If you're already financially independent from your family and have been for a while, that's great! That means that you're already half way there. The other half is taking back your power in terms of emotional leverage. If you're able to do this, you should also experience a great feeling of freedom.

Once you're able to find people who truly support you, or even better learn to utilize yourself for support, that also has an almost immediate effect. You'll finally be able to feel good about your accomplishments and be able to properly mourn your losses. Emotionally, that's going to have a big effect on your life.

Not only is getting your power back going to have an almost immediately positive effect on you, it's going to have an effect on the rest of your family as well. Now the effect on your family is not as immediate, but most of my clients express surprise at how quickly they start to see a change in their family too. For many people, just getting their power back makes a positive enough change in the way that their family treats them that they find they don't need to do anything else to improve their situation. Hopefully this will be the case with your family as well. If not, don't worry there's still a lot more we can do to motivate change in your family.

There's usually a lag from when you notice a change in yourself to when your family starts to notice this change. Once they realize that they have lost their leverage, most families feel forced to change strategies. Previously they had been using a strategy of power and control, but they can no longer do that now. When this happens, most people resort to a strategy of mutual respect.

Even if your family switches to treating you with mutual respect, it doesn't mean that they will now be a perfect family. I think you understand that perfection is not possible anyways. Even if they are not perfect, at least they will no longer be abusive. I think that you will agree that having a life free from familial abuse is worth the initial hardship.

Backlash

In some cases, but not always, there will be a backlash. Dysfunctional families tend to be resistant to change. As much as they bitch and complain, they actually like the status quo. Do you remember Melody from the beginning of the chapter? Once she started making moves towards greater independence her mother freaked-out.

This doesn't always happen, but if you are afraid it will in your case, then it's a good idea to have a plan in place. If you think there might be a more serious backlash, you should have a "go bag". A Go Bag is a backpack or duffle bag that has everything you need if you ever had to leave in a hurry. It should have important documents like your birth certificate and passport. It should also have things in it that are important to you and you "can't replace". If you have room for toiletries and some clothes, include those but keep in mind that you can purchase more of those easily if you need to.

Most of the time, the backlash appears as more social or emotional aggression. Remember Bill, the artist? When he started making moves towards more independence his father responded by sending me an email to try to discredit Bill to his own therapist. Of course, all it accomplished was to make Bill's father look bad, but it's still upsetting when these things happen.

A common tactic is to start complaining about you to the rest of the family. When this happens we usually find out about it because those family members will then come to us and say something like "Stop being so mean to mom!" If this happens, just respond to them matter-of-factly. For example "It's not my intention to be mean to mom. Right now I'm working on being more independent. This is something that I'm doing for me." Stay calm and don't offer any lengthy explanation. Keep it short and sweet.

If there is a backlash, it is usually only temporary. It is just a symptom of your family stubbornly refusing to change and trying to get you to go back to the old arrangement. Do you remember when I told you that you had to be more stubborn than your family? This is that moment. Once they realize that you are more stubborn than they are, they will usually back down.

I will be talking more about how to deal with backlash in later chapters, so hold tight if this becomes a serious problem for you.

Conclusion

I am so proud of you! Just by reading this far into the book, you have shown a commitment to taking yourself out of the equation and taking your life back. That commitment, as well as a stubborn refusal to be mistreated or controlled any longer, is really what is ultimately going to be responsible for your success in this matter. It's not easy, but if you have the will and determination to follow through, I know you can do it.

Power and control define the relationships within dysfunctional families. Certain family members seek leverage from others in order to have this control. This is why it's so important that you remove this leverage in order to end the cycle of dysfunction within your family.

It's understandable that you don't want to think of your family as being toxic and controlling. After all, families are supposed to be about mutual respect, love, and support. You want to hold on to the hope that your family can be this way without having to make major changes in the way you interact with them. It's only natural that you would feel this way. But we also have to accept the reality of the situation.

Waiting for things to change is not going to cause change to happen. If we want things to change, we have to change them. There's no way around it. True, we can't change other people or force them to change, but we can control the amount of influence they have in our life. One of the biggest ways that we can control that influence is by removing the amount of leverage other people have over us.

Maybe you're still skeptical that your family is using financial favors and emotional extortion as leverage. One of the ways you can test this is by removing that leverage and seeing how the person responds. In normal families, if an adult child says that they want to take over payments of a bill, parents are usually over-joyed. In a dysfunctional family it is seen as negative because it takes away from that power.

When you start to make changes that are designed to help you live a more independent and healthier life, take careful note of the way that your family reacts. Are they helping you or hindering you? The good news is that this backlash is usually only temporary. If not, we'll discuss in later chapters steps you can take to improve the situation.

5

Rewriting the rules

Brian is the middle child with an older brother and younger sister. When he was three years old, his father died in a motorcycle accident. Although his older brother, who was 7 when his father died, remembers him, Brian doesn't remember his father at all. He doesn't know the details about how his father died, only that his mother is angry about it and that the last time any of them had contact with his father's side of the family was at his father's funeral.

Shortly after his father's death, Brian's mother started dating almost immediately. While she was out, Brian's brother Brendan was supposed to be babysitting him, but most of the time Brendan would leave to go play with his friends and Brian was left alone in the house. Looking back, it's amazing that Brian survived his childhood. He credits this experience of essentially always having been on his own with why he has always been a capable and self-reliant person. His mother never had to nag him to do chores or do his homework. He always got himself ready for school in the morning and on the school bus without his mom having to do anything.

When he was school-aged, his mother started dating a married man at work. Although it had always seemed like his mother was too busy for them, the neglect only got worse when this relationship started. Unlike the other men she had dated, this one was long-term. A couple years into the relationship, his mother had a child with this man, Brian's little sister Brittney. Brian discovered the man his mother was dating was married because he over-heard his mother talking to a friend about it. Adults, especially in his family, often said things in Brian's presence that were inappropriate. It was as if they didn't even notice he was there even though he was out in the open and not trying to hide his presence at all.

There were many other instances where it was as though Brian was invisible, too many list here. There were times that Brian's mother forgot him at the grocery store and actually went home without him. Just about every time Brian went to the mall with his mother, he would stop briefly to look at something and when he turned around his mother was gone. Brian's mother was so careless with him that mall security was practically on a first-name basis with him. To this day, Brian has an intense fear of being lost or going somewhere unfamiliar.

Brian remembers one event from his childhood that describes what it was like to be in his family perfectly. By this point, his mother had been having the affair with the married man for several years. Their relationship was still a secret and the man had made no moves to divorce his wife. He and his wife were hosting a Christmas party at their house. Brian's mother was not invited for obvious reasons and she was furious about it. She felt that it should be her house and her Christmas party. She decided to go to it uninvited and even brought all three of her children with her.

Thankfully, Brian's mother mostly behaved herself, but there were several tense moments when Brian was afraid that there would be a confrontation between his mother and the wife. Fortunately, that didn't happen that day. While they were all standing together off to the side, the wife came over to greet them. She introduced herself and then asked Brian's mother to tell her something about each of her children. Brian's mother smiled and said "Oh, this is Brendan. He is very smart and gets good grades in school. I think he'll be a lawyer one day. And this is Brittany. She's my little Princess. She's very artistic and creative. And this is Brian. He's umm... Well, there's not much to say about Brian."

The wife looked at Brian with a look of both pity and compassion for him. She was obviously taken aback that his mother would say that about him. He just stayed quiet as usual and didn't say anything. He wasn't sure how he felt about the wife's reaction; if it made him feel better or if it made him feel worse. He also felt confused about his mother statement. I mean, how artistic can his 4 year old sister really be? Also, his older brother got bad grades in school, not good. Brian was the one who got good grades. How come she couldn't see that? How was it that a stranger was able to show more compassion and concern towards him than his own mother?

Brian's siblings grew to have their own problems. As his brother got older, he became more and more of a delinquent. It seemed that Brendan and his mother were constantly getting into fights, which led to the police frequently showing up to the house. Brendan dropped out of school at 16 and ran away from home. They didn't hear from him until several years later. Brittany was spoiled and often acted entitled and bratty. Brian was the good son who worked hard at school and used the money he earned from his after-school job to help his mother with bills. And yet, he was always the disappointment.

His mother never had anything fond to say of him. His siblings picked up on this and made fun of Brian mercilessly. His mother never defended him when he was being bullied by his siblings. She seemed annoyed whenever Brian said something to remind her that he had needs too.

When Brian graduated from High School, there was no fan fair. He actually worked the day of his High School Graduation ceremony and no one objected one bit. He went to a State University and worked his way through college. He graduated with a 3.8 GPA and paid for school all by himself. Still, no one cared. His mother expressed disappointment in him having gone to a State school. He then got accepted in a local law school. Again, nothing fancy, but a good school none the less.

Brian was certain that going to law school would make his mother finally be proud of him. He was saddened when she didn't seem to notice. He graduated and got a job as a public defender. The pay was atrocious but he was happy to have a job right out of *college when so many of his classmates weren't able to get any jobs in law. His mother expressed disappointment at him having such a low-paying job. He tried finding a new job, one that would make her proud, but it was just so difficult to get hired.*

His whole life, the message he received from his family was "You are a loser. You don't count. You don't matter. Your needs are not as important as the other people in this family. In fact, how dare you even have needs? You are such a disappointment." It seemed obvious to him that he was a terrible burden on his family. He felt terrible about being such a disappointment. It seemed clear to him what he had to do: He needed to stop being a disappointment. He needed to be successful. Then his family would finally love and accept him.

Since Brian couldn't get a better job, he decided to cut out the middle man and just go into business for himself. When he told his family his plans, everyone discouraged him. They told him that he'd never make any money and just go out of business. He decided to do it anyways, and at first they seemed right. He was struggling to get clients and hardly made any money that first year. He was still a disappointment. The second year he only made slightly more than he did as a public defender. Such a disappointment. Then the third year, things started turning around for him. He had developed a good reputation. His income doubled, almost overnight. By the fourth year he had moved into a swanky downtown office and was having to turn business away because he had more work than he could handle. He raised his fees and took on some high profile clients.

Brian had achieved that success that his family seemed to have always been pushing him for. Except now, things were different. According to his family, he was too successful. They accused him of bragging, of rubbing it in their faces. They said he was no longer relatable, and because of that they rejected him even worse than they had before. Brian could not understand what had happened. Then he realized what it was: The invisible child was no longer invisible, and they didn't like that.

Like Brian, you may be starting to realize that there are unspoken rules in your family. In Brian's family, one of the rules was that he had to be the invisible child. As part of that rule, his family is allowed to mistreat him, ignore him, and exploit him as they please. As part of that rule, Brian could never make waves, he was not allowed to ever have his own needs, and he always had to put the needs of his family members over his. When he became a successful lawyer, he essentially broke that rule, and that's why his family didn't like it. He forced them to notice him, and perhaps question the way that they had always treated him.

Does this mean you have to become hugely successful and "prove them wrong"? No. That was the strategy that Brian used and it really didn't work for him. In the end, his family still rejected him. There are actually much better tactics, which will be covered in this chapter. But, before we get to that, I want to go over the common tactics that dysfunctional families often use to try to keep you in your place.

The tactics of dysfunctional families

The essential "rule" in your dysfunctional family is that you stay in whatever role they have assigned to you. This can be a confusing concept for people to understand because it often seems that your family is really unhappy with you being in that role. Like Brian, you may feel a strong push from them to be "better", only to face a backlash once you do.

Even with children who are given the role of "problem child", you would think that as much as the parents complain about the problem child that they would want the child to get better. Yet, as a therapist who has worked with these so-called problem children, I have seen parents time and time again sabotage the child's progress in therapy and go out of their way to antagonize the child, causing the child to "blow up". Then the parent triumphantly announces "See! I told you he was bad!"

As much as everyone in your family *says* that they want you to be different, they really don't. They want you to stay in that ascribed role. As much as they complain about it, they actually benefit from you being in that role. For whatever reason, it makes them feel better about their own imperfections. The tactics listed below are often employed as a way of keeping you in that role.

- **Extreme hypocrisy:** The basic definition of hypocrisy is when someone says one thing but does another. Now, we're all guilty of hypocrisy from time to time, but in dysfunctional families the level of hypocrisy can reach extremes that are almost hard to believe. They get away with murder while you can't get away with sneezing out of turn. They demand perfection but are some of the most imperfect people out there. You may be wondering in what way this is a "tactic". The way this tactic works is that the hypocrisy is so extreme, and the person operates with such conviction, that it becomes hard for you to believe. The hypocrisy is so extreme that it confuses you. You start to doubt yourself. *Is it really possible for this person to be such a hypocrite?* After a while you start to think "Maybe I've misjudged them. Maybe I'm the one who's really wrong here." You decide that you can't trust your own judgment. Once this happens, they have control over you.
- **Two-faced:** What your family shows out in public is often very different from the side of them you see once safely indoors. It's like they have two faces: The perfect angel whom everyone loves, and then the monster that only the family and a few select others know. I've witnessed this personally: Although 18-21 year olds are legal adults, it's not unheard of to have their parent call to set up their therapy appointment for them, especially if the young adult is still a student or still living at home. One such mother called me out of concern for her 20 year old daughter. She met with me and we discussed her concerns for her daughter and then set up an appointment for the daughter

to come in. I was very impressed with the mother. She knew how to speak with professionals and seemed to be a lovely person. I thought how lucky this daughter must be. After meeting with the daughter a few times, she revealed things about her mother that were shocking. As it turned out, the mother was physically and emotionally abusive to her on a nearly daily basis. Because the mother was outwardly so charming, no one ever believed the daughter. They thought she was just lying to get attention, and so no one would help her. And this is precisely why dysfunctional families use this tactic. They know that they can get away with anything because no one would ever believe you.

- **Projection:** This one is hypocrisy mixed with outright lying and is one that dysfunctional families use frequently. Essentially, they accuse other people of doing the exact things that they themselves do. They do this with such frequency and predictability that one can often use it as a way of revealing what their family member is secretly up to. Classically, they accuse you of doing to them the exact thing that they are doing to you. So, if they accuse you of doing drugs and there's no reason why they would even suspect that, you can often deduce that actually they are the ones doing drugs. For the person on the receiving end, it is incredibly frustrating. I think the reasoning behind this tactic is to both divert attention away from themselves and to enrage the other person. Again, it's such extreme hypocrisy that it makes you question if it's even possible for a person to be this hypocritical. It is. And it's so enraging to be accused of something that they are actually doing that it can easily cause a person to lose emotional control. When you flip out, then they can then say "See, I told you he was crazy!" This is a double-win for them.

- **Nit-picking:** We all have flaws and imperfections. It's a part of being human and is nothing to be ashamed about. Normal rational people notice these little flaws in other people and ignore them. Dysfunctional people bring great attention to them and constantly nit-pick them. The idea is that they want you to feel that you can never do anything right. They want you to feel insecure to the point that you shy away from other people. In other words, they want you to feel that you must rely on their advice when it comes to making your own decisions. They want you to feel so self-conscious that you don't socialize outside of the family. The less supports you have, the easier it is to control and influence you.

- **Shaming:** This goes along with nit-picking. In functional families, when people experience misfortune or have embarrassing moments, the family supports that person and tries to help the person move past it. In dysfunctional families, the goal could be described as the opposite of "moving on". Rather they remind the person of the event years later. For instance, an adult child may be reminded of embarrassing things that happened to them in High School. The dysfunctional family also shows little tact by bringing up the incident in front of others, such as your friends or coworkers. They also gossip about these events to other family members. Rather than make a mistake and move past it like most people do, you are repeatedly shamed. The purpose of this tactic is to give you the message "You are not perfect either". It makes you hesitate to question the things your family is doing for fear that they will bring up your own short-comings in retaliation. It makes you question if you even have a right to speak-up given how "shameful" you are.

- **Ignoring boundaries:** Boundaries are basically the rules we have for how people interact with us. A basic boundary is "You don't walk in on me while I'm in the bathroom". Everyone has boundaries. If you ever quit a job or broke-up with someone, it's probably because they violated your boundaries. Some people have more strict boundaries than others. Dysfunctional families are often characterized by their lack of boundaries. People in these families show a lack of respect and consideration for each other. They expect to always be "the exception to the rule" and feel that boundaries shouldn't apply to them because they're family. They may also show a lack of boundaries by blurring the parent/child role. Children may be privy to adult information, parents may expect to be taken care of by their children, or children are expected to deal with things on their own rather than receive help from their parents. A possible reason for why they dislike boundaries so much is that boundaries are rules and rules limit their behaviors. Narcissists do not like having limits imposed on them. Boundary violations are also initially how sexual predators groom their victims.

- **Confusion technique:** My clients are often deeply confused by their dysfunctional families. I'm repeatedly asked things like "But why would she say that? She knows for a fact it's not true" or "But why would he do something like that? It doesn't make any sense!" Dysfunctional families often act in ways that no rational or logical person ever would. The question of course, is why. Sometimes the answer is that they are knowingly trying to confuse you. When employed successfully, the person spends so much time trying to figure out the confusing behavior that they are essentially overloaded, just like when a computer crashes. This allows the person to then get into your head. In general, if you find yourself feeling very confused by another person's behavior towards you, it is sometimes a sign that that person is trying to manipulate you. This isn't *always* the case, as some people are just simply confusing people, but it is something you should be aware of.

- **No privacy:** This is another very common tactic used in dysfunctional families. There is simply no privacy. Family members walk in on you while in the bathroom, they snoop through your things, watch you get undressed, read your diary, spy on you, and not allow you to have a private life outside of the family. I have even heard numerous accounts of bedroom doors being taken off the hinges. Yep, teenagers are not even allowed to have privacy in their bedrooms. This is often used as an excuse for monitoring the child's safety, but teenagers absolutely need privacy for reasons that I'm not even going to get into. I am also particularly troubled by parents that have no problem viewing their teenage or adult child naked. There are two reasons why lack of privacy in a family is so concerning. One reason is that it may be used by sexual predators to groom their victims. Another reason is that it gives the message "There's no escape!" You can't have anything outside of this family, not even privacy.

- **Divide & conquer:** Why was this Julius Caesar's favorite strategy? Because it's highly effective. Smaller groups are easier to conquer than larger groups. A united front makes for a more formidable opponent than a divided one. In the case of a dysfunctional family, the narcissist works to keep the family divided. Typically they target and isolate one person at a time. Other people in the family often realize what's going on but don't help the targeted person for fear that they will be next. This is how it's possible for just one narcissist can take control of an entire family.

- **Destroying things you love:** Abusive people often try to destroy your friendships and relationships because it's easier to dominate you when you are without supports, but it's also not uncommon for them to destroy physical things. We all have material things that we love. Perhaps you have a piece of artwork that you created and are really proud of it, maybe you have an outfit that makes you feel attractive, or some other thing that you love. We all have items or possessions that are special to us and touch our hearts. Abusive people will often destroy these items in a fit of rage. Why? Because they don't want us to be able to experience joy outside of what they can control. They feel a need to have that much control over us.

- **Splitting:** Splitting is like divide & conquer but slightly different. Splitting is when you turn two people or two groups of people against each other. Commonly this is done by feeding each person negative information about the other. The most common example is someone who says "so-and-so said this about you" or "so-and-so was so mean to me!" These are usually lies or exaggerations designed to make you dislike the other person. They then go to the other person and say the same thing about you. Now the last thing they want is for you to go to so-and-so and tell them what they said about them. If the two people start to communicate freely with each other, usually the plan falls apart because they both realize that the person was just lying and trying to manipulate them. As usual, communication is your friend.

- **"You're crazy!":** Now I know that some people say "you're crazy!" in a joking or loving way, and that's okay. I'm talking about instances when someone accuses you of being crazy and they are trying to convince you that you are actually insane or mentally unwell. In those situations it is absolutely emotional abuse. It is emotional abuse to use psychiatric terms (especially demeaning ones like "paranoid", "obsessed", and "delusional"). It's one thing if the person has an actual mental health condition (as diagnosed by a professional, not by you) and you are using these terms in the process of trying to help this person. It's another situation entirely when using these terms in order to hurt the person. Like the confusion technique, it can also be used to control the person. If you succeed in convincing the person that they are crazy, then you can get them to believe just about anything.

- **Blame:** The narcissist takes no ownership and no responsibility. They are 100% blameless and you are completely to blame for everything. They seek to either give the impression of being *so superior* to other people or *such victims* of society. Other people are always to blame for their problems, even when other people were not involved. If they got into a car accident, it's your fault for having stressed them out the day before. One client even told me about how his father blamed his alcoholism on his children. Supposedly the man had been sober for years, yet still blamed his children for having been so demanding as to turn him into an alcoholic!

- **Minimization:** Minimization can take many forms. Sometimes narcissists minimize their contribution to a conflict. They often minimize how you should feel about something they did. As noted in the previous chapter, they minimize your joy and your pain. It would seem that the goal here is to keep everything that you experience as neutral and even-keel as possible. Meanwhile, you have probably noticed that their own experiences are maximized. When it comes to them, every inconvenience is a tragedy and every positive is a brag-worthy triumph. The goal here is for you to become convinced that they are more important and to keep your stuff to yourself in order to not steal the spotlight from them.

- **Lying:** Narcissists lie so much that it can be hard to believe that a person could be capable of lying that much. Although the lies themselves are often not that clever, they say them with such certainty and conviction that it's hard not to believe them. And because they repeat the same lie over and over again, after a while you feel forced to believe it. The lies can be so outlandish and so improbable, yet said with such consistency and conviction, that you actually believe them. The result of this is that after a while you don't know what the truth is anymore. You don't know what to believe and feel as though you can't trust your own "gut instinct". You no longer know what's fact or fantasy. You feel afraid to speak up because you are no longer sure of yourself.

- **Set-ups:** Essentially, the person knowingly puts you in difficult situations. They knowingly set you up for failure.

They may repeatedly insist that you do something that they know will either be uncomfortable or humiliating for you. They may also put you in awkward social situations where you are made to be "the bad guy". Frequently you are put in a place of being the go-between between two feuding family members.

You probably noticed that most of these tactics have to do with you doubting your own judgment or feeling like you could never get by without your family. Ultimately the goal of these tactics is to dominate and control you. They want to keep you in your part of the equation. That's how they win. Naturally this can be a very confusing experience for the person experiencing it. My hope is that you will become familiar with these tactics so that you can recognize them when they are used against you.

I remember one client I had named Cara. Cara had a very dysfunctional family whom had been using these tactics against her for her entire life. Cara herself was shy, passive, introverted, but overall a very sweet person. Physically, her appearance was lovely but she was extremely self-conscious of the way she looked.

Cara had an older sister whom Cara adored despite the fact that the older sister was often cruel to her. Still, Cara admired her and would try to hang out with her and be her friend. Starting at about the age of 10, her sister started making fun of the way Cara walked. She tormented her about her gait and even enlisted her friends to make fun of her as well.

I should note that there was absolutely nothing wrong with the way Cara walked. She didn't have a limp, nor had there ever been anything wrong with the way she walked. She walked perfectly normal. Yet her sister made fun of her about her walk starting at age 10 until present. Even as an adult she was still making fun of the way she walked.

Her sister making fun of the way she walked was so consistent, so persistent, and so completely unprovoked, that Cara decided her sister must be telling the truth. It seemed especially true since her sister had gotten other people to make fun of her about it too and her mother never reprimanded her sister. Her mother never once said "Stop saying that! Your sister walks normal!" Instead, her mother would just stay quiet about it, almost as if she was agreeing with it or perhaps even ashamed of Cara's gait.

This was the beginning of Cara becoming extremely self-conscious. She watched herself walk in front of a mirror. She often looked down at her feet when she walked. She certainly never went to any dances and lost her confidence when it came to other physical activities that involved using her legs. She could never see what her sister was talking about, but instead of dismissing her sister's lies, she instead decided that she couldn't trust her own judgment. It made her wonder what else was wrong with her that she just couldn't see.

Once Cara started doubting herself, other family members took full advantage of this weakness. They picked and picked and picked until Cara was a depressed and anxious shell of a person. Her family used other tactics too, too many to mention, but you can see how just one of these manipulations can really injure a person over time. It is the very definition of cruelty and emotional abuse. This is the perfect example of how these tactics can be used to gain control of a person.

"But is it really intentional?"

No one wants to think of their family as intentionally hurting and manipulating them. When working with clients, a question I frequently get is "But is it really intentional?" They want to know if it's possible to unintentionally of unconsciously manipulate some-one. They'll often say "Perhaps my family member is just mentally ill and doesn't realize what they are doing."

It's definitely possible for people to hurt someone uninten-tionally. I know that I have certainly had plenty of experiences where someone was hurt by something I did or said and I really didn't mean to upset them at all. It does happen. But the question is: is it happening with your family now? I can't answer that question. I can tell you that by its very definition, manipulation is something done with intention and careful planning. I also do not know of any particular mental illness that would account for persistent but unintentional manipulation.

I cannot tell you if your family is using these tactics intentionally or not. However, I will encourage you to be aware of these tactics so that you can end the cycle of self-blame and self-criticism. I also want you to be aware of them so that you can employ your own tactics in order to defend yourself. Fortunately, these strategies work whether your family is intentionally being cruel to you or not. What's also good about the strategies I'm going to explain to you is that they do not involve manipulation or bullying.

Rewriting the rules

The first and most essential skill I'm going to teach you is how to set boundaries with your family. Remember, boundaries are essentially the rules we have for allowing people to interact with us or be in a relationship with us. What I need you to do is come up with a list of basic boundaries you have as well as the consequences you will have if someone violates them. In a moment, I'm going to provide you with a list of sample boundaries and consequences.

The consequences are important because they enforce the boundaries. Many of my clients think they have boundaries with their family but they really don't because they never enforce them. And by the way, "complaining" about a boundary violation is not enforcing it. If you don't enforce your boundaries, you don't act-ually have any.

This may be a difficult concept to understand, so let's use me as an example. As a therapist, I have very clear boundaries with my clients. Before anyone ever comes into my office, they are first given my office policies. My office policies are also on my website. These office policies are a written document of my boundaries. It lists what I expect from my clients and what they can expect from me. It also lists consequences for violating these boundaries. For example, if you give me less than 24 hours' notice before cancelling your appointment, you must pay a cancellation fee or you will not be given another appointment. Clients sign a contract agreeing to my boundaries at their very first session.

When I was first starting out in private practice, I felt timid enforcing this cancellation fee. I would tell people "Its okay. I'll just put you in for next week". I would tell people they didn't have to pay the fee because they had a good excuse or because it was their first time cancelling. Because of this, clients were cancelling on me last-minute all the time.

At first I was really puzzled by this. I thought to myself "Why does this keep happening? I have the 24 hours' notice rule clearly stated and people even sign a contract promising that they will agree to it!" After being in private practice for 5 years, I had never cancelled on a client with less than 24 hours' notice, so I knew that the rule was reasonable. Then I realized that I couldn't say I had a rule if I wasn't willing to reinforce it. I started charging my cancellation fee every time, no exceptions. I also found that when I reminded people of the fee when they called to cancel that most people would decide not to cancel their appointment after all. My cancellation rate went down in a hurry.

I'm not telling you that you need to write down all of your boundaries into a document and have your family sign a contract agreeing to follow them, although that may be a good idea in some cases. What I'm asking is that you decide on what those boundaries are, write them down for your own reference, and then make sure that you always follow through with the prescribed consequences. You will be surprised how quickly your family catches on.

Here is a list of example boundaries and consequences. You can use these if you feel that they work for you. You can also add to my list. The idea behind the consequences is that they prevent the person from violating your boundaries. When doing this, it's good to remind the offender of your boundary, warn them of the consequence for violating it, and then follow through with the consequence if they persist:

- You will speak to me with respect. If not, then I will hang up the phone or walk away from you.
- Disrespectful emails will be ignored and deleted immediately.
- Phone calls received after 9pm will be allowed to go to voicemail. I will only call back if the voicemail states that there is a genuine emergency.
- If you make fun of me at a family gathering, I will go home immediately.
- I will not respond to emails where you complain to me about Dad. Your marital problems are between you and Dad and I will not be the go-between.
- If you wish to borrow money from me in an amount greater than $50 then we will first have to create a written and signed contract where you agree to a repayment schedule including penalties for failure to repay within the allotted time.
- If you tell embarrassing stories about me to my friends then you will no longer be invited to spend time with me and my friends.
- If you threaten me or physically touch me in anger, I will call the police immediately and I will press charges.
- If you continue to make harassing phone calls, I will file harassment charges with the police and will seek a restraining order.
- I will not have dinner with the family if it will be used as a forum to criticize or gang up on me. If this happens I will leave immediately and may not go to future dinners.
- I will not go to your Christmas party if you invite my ex-wife.
- My decision / life choices are not for debate. If you criticize or challenge these choices I will first ask you to stop, but if you continue then I will leave.

Boundaries are the most effective if reinforced immediately. If you allow your family to gang up on you for an hour before leaving the situation, it's less effective than if you left immediately. Ideally what you want to do is give the person a warning at the first sign of mistreatment and then hang-up the phone or walk away immediately if they continue.

Many clients have expressed to me a belief that by walking away instead of fighting it out that you are letting the other person "win". I strongly disagree with this sentiment. The only way to win is to not play the game. By no longer playing the game and leaving the situation, you are in fact winning here and the perpetrator knows it.

Although it may seem like they are winning when you have to leave in the middle of Thanksgiving dinner, and they may even have a smug look of self-satisfaction on their face when you do, they are not winning. They win when you continue to passively sit through Thanksgiving dinner while they torment you. They win even more if you get sick of it and "fight back". Then they can spin it to make it look like you were "the bad one" or "crazy person". When you "fight back", they always win.

When you calmly hang up the phone or walk away, you win. You are showing the person that in this situation you have the power. You can walk away or hang up the phone and there's nothing they can do about it. In this situation, you are demon-strating to them that you have more power than they do. Remember, to narcissists and dysfunctional families, power is everything. You are also making it unlikely that they will violate your boundaries again because they know now that they can no longer get away with it. You win.

People have asked about certain situations where enforcing boundaries can be difficult. You may be wondering about these situations as well. People often ask me, "What if I walk away and they follow me?" The first time you do this; this very well may happen because the person is not familiar with your new boundary. If this happens, you then say calmly "If you continue to follow me and do not give me space, then I will be forced to get in my car and leave." You then follow that with "Because you did my respect my request, I am now leaving". You should specify if you plan to come back and if you know when you are coming back in order to show courtesy and basic respect. Remember, this is not about being passive aggressive or taking petty revenge.

Another question is "What if I can't leave?" For this reason, you should always have an escape plan. If you are going to a family gathering with someone, make sure that person knows that you may have to leave suddenly and make sure they are in agreement with this. At least for now, I would not advise going anywhere with your family if you cannot leave easily. This also means that I would advise against hosting such family gatherings because it is a lot harder to force someone out of your house than to simply walk out of someone else's home or public place.

Another question is "What if I'm driving while it happens?" True, if you're in the middle of driving you can't just walk away. However, you can pull over and tell the person that you will not start driving again until they calm down or stop the boundary violation. Let them know that if they continue that you will no longer be providing them with rides and that they will have to find their own transportation. Do not kick the person out of your car and leave them stranded unless the person represents a true danger while you are driving. At least try to get them home or to their destination as it is cruel to simply leave someone stranded if you can avoid it.

As you've probably figured out, boundaries are a lot easier to enforce if you have removed the leverage that was discussed in the previous chapter. If you have not yet succeeded in removing all of the leverage, you may not be able to enforce all of your boundaries. For instance, if your parents are still paying for your car, you probably are not in a position to refuse them transportation. Continue to work on removing this leverage and enforcing your boundaries. You would be surprised at how quickly your family will modify their behavior.

The two-sentence rule

I would like to introduce you to something I call the "two-sentence rule". The two-sentence rule is exactly what it sounds like: When expressing your boundaries, when describing your boundaries, when enforcing your boundaries, limit it to no more than two sentences.

After getting this far in the book, you may be feeling very empowered. You've gained insight about dysfunctional families, you can recognize now the tactics that they have been using against you, and you are probably feeling very righteous. For once in your life you feel very right and you may feel very tempted to prove it to the rest of your family.

Many of my clients react to this new found empowerment by getting into what I call "email wars" with their family. When a family member has violated a boundary, instead of just walking away and leaving it at that, they instead follow it up with a very long email describing the violation as well as other "evidence" of how wrong the person is. Thus begins the email war. The family member then follows suit with their very own lengthy email. And on and on it goes.

It doesn't have to be email. Sometimes it is just a very long phone call, text, or argument. This is both unnecessary and counter-productive. You will never convince your family that you are right, nor do you need to. You only need to inform them of the boundary and enforce it. You can do this in two sentences or less.

Remember, you are not an attorney trying to make a case in court. There is no judge or arbitrator that will listen to your argument and then declare "You're right!" It's not going to happen and it is highly unlikely that you can say anything to your family that will make them decide that they are wrong. However, if it is possible for them to change their mind, it is more likely that it'll be because of a two sentence remark than a long drawn out email. I'll explain why that is.

When you write a long email or otherwise give a long explanation or argument, it shows weakness. It shows that you are worked-up and emotionally charged no matter how well you think you are hiding it. It also gives the person plenty of material to poke holes in your argument. Think about it, it's much easier to destroy a two page argument than it is to destroy a two sentence argument. By limiting yourself to two sentences, you show that you are confident in what you are saying and that the matter is not up for discussion. It is final and you are not going to be swayed. This is why "email wars" never work but the two-sentence rule does.

Common objections

When you start stating and enforcing boundaries, your family will probably object to it at first. This isn't always the case though. People are often surprised by how quickly their family "gets it". But in case they do object, here are some common objections they may give as well as your two-sentence response:

- **"You're being unreasonable!":** All of the examples of boundaries I listed earlier in the chapter are in fact reasonable, so you can be certain of that. But what if you are unsure? Because you want to be absolutely certain that you are in fact making a reasonable request of your family, I think it would be a good idea to talk to someone you trust about it before trying to set a boundary with your family, or anyone else. Who is the most reasonable person you know? It helps to have this person be someone outside of your family. Do you have a really great friend, spouse, or co-worker you trust with things? If so, ask them "Do you think that I'm being unreasonable by making this request of my family?" Once you've established that your request is in fact reasonable, you can give your two-sentence response to this objection: *"I disagree. I think that this is a reasonable request."* It's really that simple.

- **"But this is the way we've always done it":** This is a common objection. My clients will often say to me something like "But how can I set boundaries with my family when this is the way it's been going on for years?" Just because you allowed something in the past doesn't mean you have to keep allowing it now. People are constantly receiving new information and having new experiences. Life is always changing. We are always changing. Because of this, sometimes things need to change. When people say "But this is the way we've always done it", they're basically telling you that you are not allowed to grow and change as an individual. That's ridiculous. Given this, you can respond *"I understand that in the past I have acted a certain way, but I am letting you know that now I will not be acting that way anymore"*.

- **"We were just joking around":** This is a bizarre line of reasoning that basically states that because they did not *intend* to hurt you, you therefore cannot be hurt by what they did, and if you are hurt then you are "milking it". Weird, right? People unintentionally hurt people all the time, but having good intentions doesn't excuse you from the wrong you committed. If I unintentionally hit your car, I'm still at fault and you can still sue me for damages. I still hurt you even though it wasn't my intention to. Saying something rude and then following it up with "no offense" or "just kidding", doesn't mean that the rude thing they said to you is no longer rude. It's still rude and you are still within your right to feel offended. Regardless of intentions, people still need to take responsibility for what they do and make an effort not to commit the error again. Your response to this objection can be "Regardless of your intentions, what you said/did still hurt me. I would appreciate it if you didn't do it again."

- **"You're too sensitive":** In my opinion, this is the lamest objection ever, yet my clients seem to give it the most weight. "But Marina, what I am being too sensitive? What if they're right?" So what if they're right? There's nothing wrong with being a sensitive person. I'm a sensitive person too and I think it's what makes me a good therapist. Sensitive people are not only sensitive to their own feelings; they're frequently sensitive to the thoughts and feelings of other people too. Sensitive people are thoughtful and caring people. I make no apologies for being a sensitive person and neither should you. Also, after all the years your family has known you, shouldn't they know by now that you're a sensitive person? They need to accept that about you and get over it. Your response is *"Don't misunderstand me, I am a sensitive person"*.

- **"Mom's not going to be around forever":** Similar versions are "You only get one brother" or "What if dad died tomorrow and this is how you last spoke to him?" Basically, they try to use guilt to lull you into complacency. "Mom's not going to be around forever, so just put up with it for now so mom can enjoy the rest of her life." What they are saying is that your mother, father, sibling, whoever, has more of a right to fair treatment than you do. Everyone should be treated with respect and not be subjected to mistreatment. Therefore, what they are saying is unreasonable. A good response you can then use is *"If you are suggesting that I abandon my reasonable request, then perhaps that is unreasonable."*

- **"You hurt mom's feelings":** This objection goes something like "By setting boundaries you are being mean and are hurting my feelings." In other words, they turned it back around on you: "Oh I'm the one being mean? No, you are!" This objection is frustrating because you don't want to hurt anyone's feelings. The whole idea of setting boundaries is so that no one gets hurt or mistreated anymore. Their feelings are not more important than yours. You deserve to be happy just as much as anyone else does. Therefore, your response is *"My feelings are important too. I hope that you* can respect these boundaries so that we can improve our relationship."

- **"You need to just suck it up":** Sometimes this is also phrased as "If you want to be part of the family, you need to try harder / suck it up". Let's break this down, shall we? So, if we accept this logic, they are saying that it is your role in the family to take all of the abuse and if you want to continue to be part of the family, you need to continue to take their abuse. Of course, this doesn't go for everyone, does it? They would never "suck it up" for you, so how is this fair? I don't buy this argument. Putting up with mistreatment or abuse is not a necessary condition of being in a relationship with anyone, I don't care if they're family or not. Abuse is always wrong. A good response to this is *"I'm sorry but I can't always be the one to suck it up or try harder. Sometimes I have to stand up for myself"*.

- **"You've done bad things too":** Dysfunctional families tend to have great memories and no shame in bringing up some wrong that you committed many years ago or even while you were still a child. They hold grudges and they use them as permission to treat you however they please because you are not perfect either. Right now they are trying to bait you into an argument where you both dredge up all the wrongs the other has committed and try to prove who has done more. Even if you know for a fact that they have done worse things or many more things than you have, there's no way you can win that argument, so don't take the bait. Stay calm, cool, and collected. A perfect response is *"It's not a contest over who has hurt who more. This is about making things better moving forward"*

Remember, when you give your response, you want to stay perfectly calm, yet assertive. Try to use the same tone of voice you would use if you were to say "It's raining outside". Speak matter-of-factly. Remember, you are simply stating a fact. This is just the way it's going to be now moving forward. You're not angry, scared, or smug about it. It is what it is.

So what if your family hears your response but keeps trying to argue with you anyways? Unfortunately this is likely to happen, although perhaps not as likely as you may think. Many of my clients have expressed surprise at how quickly their family accepted their new boundaries. But in case your family does try to continue to argue with you, once again, you just give a two-sentence response *"I've said everything I'm going to say. This is not up for debate."* You then hang up the phone or walk away if they continue. It's that simple.

Conclusion

Have you ever seen the show "Super Nanny" or "Nanny 911"? If you've never seen the show or it's been a while, I want you to go watch an episode right now. If you've watched the show, you know that every episode is basically the same. Here's the gist of it: The parents have basically no boundaries with their children, or they think they have boundaries but don't enforce them. Due to this, the children are out of control. Everyone's miserable and no one's getting along.

Then the nanny shows up. She teaches the parents how to set and most importantly, enforce appropriate boundaries. The first time the parents decide to enforce boundaries (such as by giving the child a time-out), it's a disaster. At first it seems that the boundaries have made things worse. There are episodes where the child has a temper tantrum that lasts for three hours trying to avoid a five minute time-out.

But here's the beauty of it: Once the child realizes that their parents aren't budging and that their tantrum isn't going to get them anywhere, they stop. They start following the rules and suddenly things get remarkably better for the family. It seemed to get worse at first, but because the parents followed through and stuck to their guns, it got much, much better.

The same is going to be true for you. When first setting boundaries with your family, it's going to seem like it's gone horribly wrong. They are going to be resistant to the "new you" and will try everything they can to get the "old you" to come back. Once they realize that the "new you" is here to stay, they will eventually adjust their behavior.

Setting and enforcing boundaries is the most effective tool anyone can have in any relationship. I encourage you to use this tool not just with your family but with your spouse, co-workers, customers, even your boss! Learn what acceptable treatment is and what's not and start communicating this to the people who interact with you. I don't accept disrespectful behavior from anyone. Prior to being in private practice, I had no problem telling my boss that his/her behavior towards me was unacceptable. What I found was that this didn't lead to people disliking me; it actually made people actually like me more. People respected me more. People respect people that have appropriate boundaries.

Now I know that being assertive can be scary, especially if you have a long history of being passive. That's why I recommend you practice being assertive and setting boundaries with people who don't intimidate you first. Build up your confidence with these people and then work your way up to confronting your family. It can also help to have an assertive role model to reference if you find yourself unsure of what to do.

Who is the most respectable person you know? Who is the most assertive person you know? Who is the person that gets treated with respect even if other people don't necessary agree with them? That person is going to be your role model. When faced with a situation and you are wondering how you should respond, ask yourself what that person would do. If you can't think of anyone you know to serve as your role model, I often recommend people use the President as a reference. How would the President respond to your family disrespecting him? I bet he wouldn't put up with it, would he? Remember, you deserve to be treated with respect just like everyone else does.

6

The new Golden Rule

Aisha was always the one everyone could depend on. She grew up in a large family dominated by her mother and her aunts. At one point they all lived together in the same tiny apartment. Looking back, Aisha is surprised that her mother and aunts would keep getting pregnant and keep having kids when they didn't have the means or the energy to care for the kids they already had.

Aisha's mother and aunts were very similar. They all seemed to be suffering from vague but chronic medical conditions. One was forever fatigued and plagued by migraines. Another had chronic pain and an inability to focus. No doctor could ever quite pin point what the problem was, but it was suggested many times that perhaps the problem was psychological. None of them ever had a job for very long. It was just too much for them.

In addition to never having a job for long, they also never had a boyfriend for long. Aisha went through so many step-dads and step-uncles that she couldn't remember all of their names. She just remembers that each time they declared that the new man was "the one", would get pregnant by him, then declare that he was a no-good cheating woman-beating pig.

Aisha was the one that held the family together. She did the grocery shopping, picked up the younger ones from school, cooked dinner, cleaned the house, and made sure everyone did their homework. Meanwhile, her mother just lay on the couch. Did this bother Aisha? Absolutely! But seemingly, there was nothing she could do about it.

One time when Aisha was 12 she complained to her mom about having to do everything. Without warning, her mother backhanded Aisha across the face so hard that it knocked her off her feet. Aisha then tried to run away and her mother ran after her. Her mother, whom always complained of not having any energy and not being able to get out of bed, ran after Aisha with the strength and vigor of a teenager.

She cornered Aisha in her bedroom. Aisha cowered in the corner as her mother beat her with a clothes hanger. Even then she wasn't done. Aisha's mother then went into her closet and tore up some of Aisha's favorite clothes. After that incident, Aisha never questioned her mother again. Even after one of her mother's boyfriends started molesting her; Aisha still did not say anything to her mother about the sexual abuse for fear of angering her. It was clear to Aisha that she only existed to fulfill the needs of other people.

Aisha's mother stopped beating her when she became a teenager. At that point Aisha was barely home because she was working all the time and Aisha's mother must have known that Aisha was big enough now that she could fight back. Instead, Aisha's family started using her emotionally. Aisha became the emotional dumping-ground for everyone else's problems. She was constantly consoling, giving advice, and comforting the people in her family.

Aisha was a hard worker. She became the President of Human Resources at a local bank. She married an equally hard-working man and they had two beautiful children together. Aisha should have had the perfect life, but her family continued to use her as a crutch and caretaker. She was constantly giving her mother money, babysitting her nieces and nephews, and getting phone calls from frantic family members at all hours of the night.

The day finally came where for once in her life, Aisha needed a favor. She was driving home from work and another driver swerved into her lane and hit her head-on. Her car spun off the road and she was knocked unconscious. She woke up in the hospital. She was okay but she need some support as she would be *remaining in the hospital for a few days. Specifically, it would help if people could watch her kids for her. She had watched her nieces and nephews so many times that she couldn't imagine them saying "no". And yet, everyone was too busy to help her in her time of need. This really upset Aisha and her husband.*

Then when her mother came to visit her in the hospital, her mother made the whole thing about her. Instead of asking Aisha how she was, she went on a long complaining session of how her boyfriend was cheating on her again. She complained about her vague health conditions, how sick she was, etc. Aisha could not believe the nerve of her mother and told her to leave.

The next day Aisha heard that her mother was in the hospital due to a suicide attempt. Aisha felt that her mother did this because Aisha had the gall to take the attention away from her mother. The rest of her family chastised Aisha for being mean to mom and "driving her to try to kill herself". Aisha decided that she had had enough.

Both Aisha and her husband decided that they would not be doing anymore favors for her family unless things changed. For her entire life, Aisha had been sacrificing her own needs for her family. Then the one time she needs help they couldn't be bothered. She felt used and exploited and she didn't want to feel that way anymore. She decided that she would not be doing a single favor unless it was for a person who had helped her at least once in the past.

The Golden Rule states that you should treat others the way that you would like to be treated. This is a good general rule to have in life and I would recommend it to most people, but I draw the line with dysfunctional families. I'll be explaining why that is in this chapter as well as an alternative Golden Rule that I think is much more effective.

When you grow up in a dysfunctional family, you just want to be loved and treated with kindness so desperately. When despite your best efforts you don't receive this love and kindness, you get told that you just need to "try harder", "suck it up", "kill them with kindness", and "treat them the way that you would want to be treated". So you do all that hoping that they will reciprocate, but they never do.

For years and years and years you try your very best. You sacrifice things to them that no one else would ever sacrifice. You give and give and give but get nothing back in return. Or perhaps you get something, but it's very little. Like Aisha, the one time you need help, you find that you are on your own.

Why the Golden Rule doesn't work

When dealing with functional people, the Golden Rule works wonderfully. For instance, you help your new neighbor unload their moving truck and then later on they return the favor by helping you with some project you have. Functional people reciprocate.

In dysfunctional families, there is very rarely reciprocation. Rather one or a few individuals are chosen to be sacrifices to the benefit of the family. Aisha was that sacrifice. She sacrificed her childhood so that her mother could live like a Queen. Once she became an adult, she was still expected to sacrifice her free time, emotional health, and disposable income to her family.

"Killing them with kindness" will never work in a toxic and dysfunctional family. A dysfunctional family will never reciprocate because that doesn't fit into their equation. The way that they view relationships is that in any relationship some people win and some people lose, but both people can't win, and they would rather be the person that wins. That's why the Golden Rule doesn't work here.

The problem is that probably from a young age you were groomed to put the needs of others over your own. I do recognize that that isn't the case with all children from dysfunctional families. Some children were groomed to be the "winners" who got their needs taken care of at the expense of their sibling's. However, I'm going to assume that most people reading this book are like Aisha and had their needs come last.

The problem is, when you are raised to be in that role, that role doesn't end as soon as you turn 18 or move out of the family home. Without deliberate effort to change it, that role will continue to follow you. It will follow you into your adult relationships, friendships, and work environment. The Golden Rule doesn't work for people who have been being exploited all their life. For these individuals, it just leads to more exploitation.

The new Golden Rule I want you to adopt is "reciprocation". In other words, you only give what you receive. Does that mean that if you receive abuse you should give back abuse? Absolutely not! If someone starts to mistreat you, you state and enforce your boundaries; you walk away. You should always treat other people with basic respect, not because of the Golden Rule, but because you have too much respect for yourself to behave in a shameful and disgraceful manner.

Reciprocation

Aisha learned that it was poor boundaries to give so much when she received so little. She greatly scaled back the amount she was giving in order to bring it up to par with what she was getting from her family. Now, if in the future her family were to start doing more favors for her, she decided that she would start doing more too. This is reciprocation.

Reciprocation is a way to end the cycle of exploitation. I understand that a lot of people don't like the philosophy of reciprocation. They claim that it is unnatural, un-Christian, and "Imagine what the world would be like if everyone did this". I think what people forget is that in functional families, children are actually taught reciprocation from a very young age. For example: "You're brother is letting you play with his toys so you should offer to let him play with some of your toys", "Sally invited you to her birthday party so you need to invite her to yours", and "Let's not give Billy such an expensive present. His family seems to like less expensive gifts".

In functional families, parents are concerned about their child being exploited or exploiting another child. So they actively teach their children how to avoid these things. One of the ways they teach this is through teaching the importance of reciprocation. In dysfunctional families, reciprocation is either never taught or actively discouraged. One child is taught to perpetually be the "Giver" and another to always be the "Taker".

Lessons like reciprocation are usually taught at such an early age that people from functional families forget that it was something that was taught to them. The lesson is integrated and for the most part becomes "unconscious". It just *feels right* to reciprocate when someone has been kind to us and to withhold when someone has been unkind to us. It becomes second nature and after a while no longer requires conscious thought. We forget that this was actually something that was actively taught to us by our parents at a young age.

People from dysfunctional families are not taught lessons like reciprocation. For the most part, they are only taught things that correspond to the role that has been chosen for them. Because of this, they often give till it hurts. They are exploited, not just by their family, but later by "friends", significant others, and co-workers.

It is poor boundaries in any relationship to be the one who always "gives". So, reciprocation is part of improving your boundaries with your family as well as others. This conscious and deliberate measuring of give-and-take within relationships isn't something that you're going to necessarily have to do for the rest of your life. However, if reciprocation is something that you have struggled with in the past, I think it's a good idea to follow it as closely as possible for at least the next year. Once you get into the habit of it and have fully ended the cycle of exploitation, you can try to take a more natural approach to your relationships with other people and see how that goes. If you find yourself being exploited again, then you can go back to reciprocation.

The basic rule of reciprocation is not to give more than you get. Some of my clients are such givers that they will even go so far as to allow someone they hardly know to live with them. They give so much of themselves only to have the person never reciprocate. Some of these people they give so much to end up taking even more on top of what they were already given. I have seen these acts of kindness go very wrong in the end.

Therefore, when someone is asking a favor of you or you're considering offering a favor, ask yourself "Has this person done me a similar favor or a favor of equal value?" If the answer is no, then you should say "no" or simply not make the offer. Now it could be that the person is experiencing unusual or special circumstances and so they have been unable to do you a similar favor in the past because the nature of the situation is so unique. In situations like this, ask yourself "If we had switched roles and I was the one in need and he was in a position to help me, would he?" Think long and hard about this. You want to look at the situation realistically, not optimistically. If the answer is "unlikely", then don't do the favor. If you don't know the person well enough to answer any of these questions, then the answer is always "no".

It's usually after explaining all of this that a client will ask me "But what if I'm this person's only hope?" Indeed, it's in the interests of manipulators, con men, and scammers to convince you that you are the only one who can help them. But are you really? I already explained in Chapter 4 that it's actually highly unlikely that you would be anyone's last hope or even best option. Even if someone truly doesn't have any of their own capabilities and no family, they most likely have other people or government agencies that they can turn to for assistance. If someone truly has no one but you, that's telling you a lot. You have to burn a lot of bridges in life in order to end up in a situation where you only have one person left who can help you. Perhaps it's best not to get involved with someone who has burned so many people.

Also, promises of future acts of reciprocation don't count. When deciding how much or how often to reciprocate, only use the things that have already happened as a guide. There are plenty of people out there who say "Just do me this one favor and I'll promise you that the next time you need something I'll be the first one to volunteer" but when the time comes they are nowhere to be found. If this sounds cold, then I want you to think back to how many times someone promised you they would "pay you back" but then either never did or it took a lot of wrangling to make it happen. What would you say your "pay-back" rate is? Would you put it at 50% or perhaps even less than that? This is why at least for now I don't want to count any of these promises until they've actually happened.

Another thing that is important to remember is that exploitation isn't always about the big cons. More often than not, exploitation occurs inch by inch and little by little. The kinds of people that exploit other people are always on the lookout for people that they believe would be easy victims. For them, the perfect victim is someone who is a people-pleaser and has a very giving nature. In other words, they are looking for people with poor boundaries. Sometimes I think these exploiters can tell just by looking at people that they are "givers". Other times I think that they just cast a wide net and see who falls in.

Let's first start with the theory that people can "just tell" you're an easy target. As a petite woman, I have lots of experience with this. Living in the city, I've been mugged and approached by creeps more times than I would care to admit. I finally decided that I should get a license to carry mace. Since getting my mace, I have not been mugged or bothered by creeps even once. The interesting thing about this is that there's no way for them to know that I have mace. It's either kept in my purse or my coat pocket. So why the change? I believe it's because I probably act differently when I have the mace. I probably come off as less fearful and more confident. This makes me think that if exploiters can "just tell", then maybe they are just more keen to subtle clues that have to do with confidence more than anything. This is good news because it means that all we have to do is to stop thinking of ourselves as victims and we'll most likely decrease the incidences of us being seen as targets.

Another possibility is that exploiters cast a wide net. They simply leave out the bait and see who has poor enough boundaries to fall for it. I saw an example of this once while I was waiting for the bus. There were several of us sitting there waiting for the bus to come when a haggard looking woman approached. The woman didn't look homeless, but she did look like she possibly had a drug problem. She walked up to me and said "Can I ask you a favor?" Without looking up from my book I said "No" and kept reading. I then watched her ask other people the same thing. Some people didn't answer her at all, but rather simply ignored her. Other people said "yes", but then said no to her request for money. She was asking for a dollar. Then I saw a young woman take the bait and give her a dollar. She then asked the woman for more money. Now the story was that she really needed $20. The woman would not leave her alone. She gave her another $2 which I imagine was a sort of "go away fee", but this just encouraged the woman even more. She wouldn't leave her alone until the bus came.

And this is how it works. They test people's boundaries to see who will give in, and then once they know who has the poor boundaries, they go further. This is how poor boundaries leads to exploitation. Like I said, it often starts small. Asking a stranger to do you a favor is showing poor boundaries. Now, it's one thing if you're stranded and just needed to use someone's phone real quick, but it's quite another situation to be doing what that woman was doing.

Since we know that larger boundary violations often start small, I want you to pay attention to even small instances of reciprocation that in the past you wouldn't have thought was a big deal. The young woman at the bus stop probably didn't think it was a big deal to give someone $1, but it then lead to her being harassed by a stranger for ten minutes. Of course, it's not just strangers you have to pay attention to, but also your family.

You've probably noticed that you seem to be "targeted" more often than other people. You probably realize now that the reason for that is not because you are "cursed", but more likely due to a combination of two things. One of those things is that when we have low confidence or low self-esteem, we probably give off subtle clues that we personally are unaware of but other people can pick up on. The good news is that we can change this by changing the way that we feel about ourselves, just like how things changed for me when I started carrying mace. You don't have to carry mace to achieve the same effect, of course! And secondly, people target us through feeling-out how firm our boundaries are by attempting small boundary violations first. These small boundary violations then lead to bigger and bigger boundary violations later on.

Given that big violations start small, I want you to start paying closer attention to these small boundary violations and what they communicate to other people. For instance, let's say that you have family who frequently "forgets" about your birthday. I put *forget* in quotations because in the age of social media there are plenty of things to give them notifications that your birthday is coming up. Yet, your birthday goes by with hardly any notice. You on the other hand, always make sure to give them a card, a small gift, take them out to dinner, etc. Now, it may seem like you do this because you want to be kind, but what message could this possibly be giving your family? One of the things it communicates is that they are more important than you or more deserving of consideration than you.

One of my clients had a similar situation with Christmas and Birthday gift exchanges from his dysfunctional family. He would always spend about $50 on each family member. His family on the other hand would give him gifts that were obvious re-gifts, used items, or from the dollar store. The impression he got was that they were giving him these things just to say they had given him a gift, rather than try to give him something that he would actually enjoy. Some family members wouldn't even bother to give him anything, yet he would give them a gift every year.

On the surface he told himself that he did this just because he liked giving them nice gifts, but when he really thought about it he realized that deep down he was trying to buy their love. I advised him to give them gifts that were on par with the gifts that they had given him the previous year. Anyone who didn't give him a gift last year wouldn't get one this year. An interesting thing happened, the next year people put more effort into the gifts they gave him. He took a stand and his family actually started to respect him more.

You may be wondering about family members who can't afford nice gifts because of their financial situation. This is a gray area where there really isn't any clear answer. My question is "Does the person show appreciation?" Often times my clients tell me that the person that they are giving these nice gifts to or helping out financially actually expresses a great deal of resentment and hostility towards them. Some have even told me that the person uses their generosity against them, such as gossiping to the family that they "brag" or "shove it in their face" that they make more money than they do. Also, rationalizing to yourself "Well, I think they do secretly appreciate it, they just don't show it out of embarrassment" is not the same as them showing appreciation to you. If the person doesn't even show you appreciation, then I would say that there is a high possibility that you are being exploited.

Priorities

Sometimes reciprocation is not as easy as making sure you are not spending more money than anyone else. We also need to look at the way that we reciprocate our priorities.

We all have a sort of mental list of priorities, where things are ranked. For me, my #1 priority is my marriage. For other people it may be their career or their children. We encounter problems when we are in a relationship with someone and there is a mismatch of priorities. For instance, I would be very unhappy in my marriage if for my husband his marriage was #10 on his list of priorities. That would mean we had a mismatch in priorities and would most likely lead to one of us feeling resentful.

When you were a child, you were probably taught to put other people's needs before your own. Specifically, you were most likely taught to put the narcissist's needs at #1, followed by other family members' needs. Next on the list were things that had to do with protecting the image of the family like staying thin, looking good, doing well in school, picking a high-status spouse, etc. Your own needs then came last on the list or were not on the list at all. In order for these lists to be on par with each other, the narcissist would have had to put your needs at the top of their list and their needs on the bottom. But are they? Typically, the narcissist puts their needs first and your needs last. Because of this, we would say that these priorities do not reciprocate.

I want you to take a moment to think about your friends and family. Where would you say you fall on their lists? Where are they on your list? Is there a mismatch? You can often tell where you fall on someone's list by the amount of effort they put into maintaining the relationship. If you put in more effort than they do, then you probably have them higher on your list than they have you.

I want to give you an example of a mismatch in priorities. One of my clients, Beth, was having some problems with her in-laws. They lived in Maine and she lived here in Massachusetts. It took about 2.5 hours to drive to her in-laws' town. It was an annoying drive but still very doable. She put in the effort to have a relationship with them but her in-laws showed a mismatch in priorities when it came to scheduling visits with her.

When Beth invited the in-laws to Massachusetts for holidays or family get-togethers, she was a gracious host. She scheduled activities, had a lovely guestroom set up, bought expensive food, etc., but 9 times out of 10, the in-laws would cancel last minute. Actually, you couldn't even say it was last minute because they would call two hours after they were supposed to have arrived. When they did show up, they were hours late and not the best guests.

The few times Beth was invited to go visit them in Maine, Beth never cancelled and always showed up on time. It was apparent to her that her in-laws didn't put any effort into the visit.

They had made no plans and put no effort into any kind of entertainment. The house was dirty and the "accommodations" were a sleeping bag on the porch because they hadn't had time to set up the guest room. Beth also told me about something that we both thought that was quite odd. One time they invited Beth and her husband to come visit and when they got there, there was no one home. They couldn't get ahold of her in-laws, so they waited all day. They didn't show up to the house until late at night and acted like it was nothing.

Clearly, Beth and her husband were placing their in-laws higher on the priority list than their in-laws placed them. As Beth was learning more about assertiveness and boundaries from me, she came into conflict with her in-laws. She received an email from them inviting her to spend Christmas with them up in Maine. In previous years they had come down to Massachusetts (although they usually cancelled last minute), which allowed Beth to see both sides of the family during Christmas. This year they wanted her to arrive on Christmas Eve and then not leave until the 27th. This would mean missing Christmas with her own family and based on previous experiences with her in-laws, Beth could reliably predict that this would be an unpleasant experience as well.

Beth realized that by spending Christmas with her in-laws, she would be putting them higher on her list of priorities than her own family. This just didn't seem right given the fact that they had shown her to be so low on her own list of priorities. I helped Beth create a cordial but assertive email response to her in-laws stating basically that it wouldn't be right for her to give up Christmas with her own family when they had cancelled on her so frequently in the past.

In the end, Beth's husband went up to Maine while Beth stayed with her family here. Although Beth was afraid that her in-laws would be mad at her about the email as well as her refusal to go up to Maine, they actually weren't. After that, they started being more considerate about cancelling. Meanwhile, Beth and her husband made sure that they adjusted their priorities to be more in line with their in-laws. That way no one felt resentful or taken advantage of.

When dealing with friends or even co-workers, you want to make sure that where they are on your list of priorities lines up with where you are on theirs. So many of the people who come to me for therapy have so-called "friends" that they do favors for yet these favors are never reciprocated back. These "friends" also cancel on them frequently and don't invite them to the really good stuff they are doing. If you have any friends like this, you need to stop going out of your way for them if they're not doing the same for you. Adjust their ranking on your list so that it better lines up to where you are on theirs.

One of the common fears my clients have is that if they do this they'll find themselves with no friends. This may actually be a valid fear if you currently don't have any real friends. However, don't let this fear hold you back from doing the right thing. There's a quote by Rumi that I love that states that we shouldn't grieve the things that leave our lives because they make room for something better to come in.

When we get rid of toxic people or at least move people lower on our priority list, we make room for the people that actually deserve us and will appreciate us. You may feel lonely for a while, but eventually you will fill that emptiness with great friends and positive people. One of the ways that we are able to attract these great people is by making sure that we have our priorities straight.

I used to work in a facility where one of my responsibilities was to hold daily group therapy sessions for the residents. I was a very green therapist, but I worked with some very experienced therapists that taught me a lot. There was an older man who worked there that in my opinion was just over-flowing with wisdom. I once had the privilege of having him be my co-leader at one of these group therapy sessions.

During the group he said that so many of the problems we encounter in life are actually from not having our priorities straight. He pointed out to each person in the group how the problems they were currently experiencing in their life were actually from not putting themselves first. We sacrifice so much of ourselves to try to make other people happy, and what does it get us? As it turns out, we're not very good at making other people happy, are we?

At that time in my life, hearing his words was like a revelation. I was putting everyone else first, and what did I have to show for it? When I tried to see what my success rate was for making other people happy, it was actually quite low. Why was I putting so much time and effort into making other people happy when truth be told I wasn't even that good at it? Since we are each so much better at making our own selves happy, maybe we all should be focusing on that instead?

Of course, this doesn't mean that it's okay to be mean to other people or just completely disregard other people, but it does mean that you should be putting yourself and things that are important to you at the top of your priority list. Once you start valuing yourself like this, you would be amazed at how different you start to feel about yourself and how much better other people start treating you. Treat yourself the way you would like others to treat you, and they may just follow suit.

Conclusion

One of the ways we maintain healthy boundaries with other people is by using reciprocation and by being mindful of our priorities. Remember, having appropriate boundaries is how we can keep ourselves from being disrespected, exploited, and mistreated by others.

Some of my clients have summed up all of this to mean that we should simply follow other people's leads. For the most part I would say that this is a correct interpretation and can be a good general rule of thumb to have when interacting with other people. However, I would put a few caveats to this. No matter what, we still must treat other people with respect.

I remember one of my clients was having problems with disrespectful treatment at work. He decided that as part of his new rule of reciprocation he would then "get back at" these specific co-workers. As you can imagine, this made the situation worse, not better. I never want you to reciprocate mistreatment, disrespectful behavior, or passive aggression. I simply want you to stop doing favors and going out of your way for those people that don't do the same for you. If they are really intolerable, avoid them as much as possible, but when you do have to interact with them, remain respectful yet assertive in your interactions.

When we reciprocate bad behavior, the message we give other people is that this behavior is okay with us. Whether you realize it or not, you're saying "I'm fine with this type of interaction, so by all means, bring it on!" That's why reciprocating bad behavior only makes things worse, not better. If you don't believe me, you're free to try it for yourself and see what happens. It'll probably feel good in the moment but you'll later find that now things have gotten worse for you.

People hate it when I tell them that they shouldn't reciprocate bad behavior. They often respond by telling me a story about how when they were a kid they were bullied until they finally punched the bully in the face and that's when the bullying stopped. I had a similar thing happen in my own childhood. I was bullied mercilessly in middle school until I finally couldn't take it anymore and confronted the bullies. After that I wasn't bullied anymore and I realized that the bullies weren't as tough as I thought they were.

The "punch the bully in the face" thing worked great when we were kids, but does it really work as an adult? It seems to me that it is an immature way of handling conflict with other people. Immaturity is fine when you are a child, but doesn't look good when you are an adult. But since this is such a common objection, I'm going to take the time to really explain to you why this strategy doesn't work for adults.

Something I didn't know in middle school that I know now is why I was bullied in the first place. I was bullied, not because I was deserving of that kind of treatment, but merely because I was an easy target. I was an easy target because I had low self-esteem and didn't respect myself. I felt that other kids were better than me. I was timid and fearful and not likely to stand up for myself. As much as I tried to hide this, the bullies figured it out either through subtle clues that I didn't realize I was giving off or through testing my boundaries. Because of that, I was a target for bullies. When I finally stood up for myself I stopped being a target because I showed the bullies that I was now willing to respect myself.

Childhood bullies are similar to adult bullies in this way. As an adult, people treat you with disrespect because they pick up on the clues that tell them that you don't respectful yourself and are thus willing to put up with mistreatment from others. The reason why subjecting these bullies to the same treatment they give you doesn't work is because no self-respecting adult would act in that manner. Once again, you are showing the bullies that you don't respect yourself, thus encouraging them even more.

So, a self-respecting kid would punch a bully in the face, but a self-respecting adult wouldn't. That's the difference and that's why the tactic that worked so well as a child no longer works as an adult. So what would a self-respecting adult do? Well, for one thing, they would put themselves above such immature behavior.

A self-respecting adult would simply end their relationship with that person or avoid them as much as possible until their behavior changed. They would do their best to "walk around them" or find ways to prevent them from doing the disrespectful behavior to begin with. The few times they did have to interact with them, they would be cordial, diplomatic, and assertive. They would be above the fray.

And that's really the point of all this: so that you are no longer a target and no longer exploited. You follow other people's leads, but you also don't sink to their level. In doing so, you maintain your self-respect. This is both true with your family, as well as with others.

7

Low Contact

Michael had been taught that as a man, he always had to do the right thing and if he made a mistake, then he needed to man-up and take ownership of it. At 18 years old he enlisted in the Navy and was excited at the prospect of serving his country as well as gaining what he saw as valuable life experiences and discipline. He took well to the structure of the military and looking back, considers it to be among the best years of his life.

Michael found himself stationed at a Naval base Stateside. He and the boys would often go into town for an evening of drinking, dancing, and meeting girls. It was then that he met Liz. His impression at the time was that the relationship was very casual. She was dating other men and didn't seem to want any kind of commitment. They did have sex however. Just one month into their "relationship", Liz informed him that she was pregnant and that he was the father.

Michael was torn. He's only known this woman for a month and he knew for a fact that during this time she had been sleeping with other men. It's possible that the child is his but also very likely that it was someone else's. He was also only 20 and wanted to focus on his naval career. At the same time, he had a strong belief in "manning up" and "doing the right thing".

Michael received pressure from both sides. Liz was laying the guilt on him, as was her father. He knew that if they did end up together, it would be a bad thing that he had made her beg him while she was pregnant. Meanwhile, his own family was excited about there being a baby and wanted him to marry Liz. Michael *eventually relented and married Liz before the baby was born. She named the baby Michael Junior.*

Michael did not re-enlist and instead took a civilian job. He bought a home and took care of everything. Michael went to work and Liz took care of the home and baby. At first everything was fine. It wasn't ideal, but they seemed to have a happy little family together. Michael was working too much to really notice that things weren't quite right. He realized later that his wife had a shopping addiction and also a problem with alcohol.

Liz would drain Michael's bank account and if he tried to confront her about it, she would fly off into a violent rage. When Liz was unhappy, it was like living in Hell. Yet, Michael felt trapped. Junior was still young and he worried about the scandal of divorcing so soon into the marriage and while his son was still so young. He tried his best to appease Liz and just wait until Junior was old enough so he could divorce her. He buried himself in his work so he could avoid her as much as possible.

Liz must have caught on to Michael's plan because as soon as Junior was old enough, she was pregnant once more. Michael was convinced that Liz was sabotaging the birth control, but what could he do? Liz was pregnant once again 5 years later. Now he had a family of three and had already spent 10 years of his life in an unhappy marriage. He stopped having sex with Liz after that. Liz did not complain, but she did continue drinking and compulsively shopping.

When Michael's youngest was 7, Michael was confronted by a woman who lived in his town. The woman told him that Liz was having sex with her husband and that she wanted Michael to know this and would appreciate it if Michael could get Liz to stop. For Michael, this was the final straw. He could only put up with so much. Were any of his kids his? It was then that he got a divorce from Liz.

At this time his son Junior was 18. Liz got custody of the two youngest but Junior decided to live with his dad. During this time, Michael found out a lot of things about his marriage from Junior that he didn't know since he worked so much. Junior was surprised that his father didn't know that Liz had basically cheated on him throughout his marriage. Junior also revealed that she had treated the children poorly as well. Michael and Junior at first seemed to bond over their shared mistreatment at the hands of Liz.

After this honeymoon period was over, Michael began to notice things about Junior that were similar to his ex-wife. Junior never could seem to get a job and instead just "minded the house". He drank a lot too and seemed to always be borrowing money from dad. If Michael said anything about Junior getting a job, Junior would fly into a rage. These rages became more and more frequent.

If Michael tried talking to Junior about being his own man and working towards getting his own place, Junior would throw it back in his face that Michael never wanted him to be born and thought he wasn't his real son. Those were things that Michael never wanted Junior to know, but unfortunately Liz had told Junior these things in an effort to make Michael look bad and turn his son against him. Once again, Michael was torn. He wanted to help his adult son, but he also knew that the things Junior was doing weren't right.

As the years went by, there were times where it looked like Junior was getting his life together and showed promise. Junior would do job training or meet a nice girl. Junior would find an apartment and start acting more independent. Then, things would slide back to the way they were. Junior took advantage of everyone he could. Michael suspected Junior was doing other drugs in addition to being an alcoholic. He tried and tried and tried, but nothing ever helped Junior and Junior was never even appreciative of his father's efforts.

For years, Michael tried to convince Junior to see a therapist. Every time he made this suggestion, Junior would say that it was actually he who needed to see a therapist. Michael heard this so many times that he decided that at least one of them should go see a therapist, so he went ahead and scheduled an appointment for himself.

Through therapy, Michael realized that he needed to stop doing so much for Junior. Junior was well into his adult years now and Michael had done enough for him. It was up to Junior to start making better choices or to start accepting responsibility for the choices he was making. Michael needed to have better boundaries with Junior, which meant no more giving Junior money or allowing him to live with him when he got evicted or kicked-out by his girlfriend.

Michael also set boundaries with Junior in regards to treating him with more respect. One of the problems that Michael encountered though is that a drug addict can rarely be depended upon to follow boundaries. Michael frequently found himself having to cut visits short, hanging up the phone, etc. Despite having firm boundaries with Junior, he was still getting a lot of abuse from him, yet Michael was not willing to completely cut off his son.

Michael's therapist helped Michael to create enough "distance" between him and his son that the possibility of mis-treatment or abuse was greatly decreased. Michael was still able to have some contact with his son, but less enough that Junior didn't feel capable of taking advantage of his dad. Meanwhile, Michael started spending more time with his two adult daughters. They had both grown into lovely people and supported his decision to have low contact with Junior.

Through his relationship with his daughters and their children, Michael was finally able to have that loving family he always wanted. Would he have preferred to have included Junior in all of those moments as well? Absolutely! But he was learning that he had to look at the situation realistically rather than how he hoped it would be. By being realistic and accepting the situation for what it was, he was now able to have more positive experiences with his family than not, and to him that was much better than the alternative.

If you have successfully followed through with removing leverage, setting and reinforcing boundaries, reciprocating, and resetting your priorities, most of the people reading this book will already be starting to see an improvement with their dysfunctional family, and they will see even more of an improvement as time goes on. However, for someone like Michael, doing all of that will still not be enough.

Another possibility is that you have started to implement all of the skills listed in previous chapters and your family is now rebelling against. They are doing everything they can to try to convince you to go back to the "old you". In most cases, this rebellion will be only temporary; however it can help to decrease the contact you have with them during this time.

In the next two chapters I'm going to introduce you to two new terms. One is "low contact" and the other is "no contact". For now, we are going to focus on low contact. Low contact is simply decreasing the amount of contact you have with your dysfunctional and toxic family. In the process you also decrease your availability to them and "create distance". How low you go is up to you. I'll be providing you with information regarding how to determine how low you need to go.

Creating distance

One of the common characteristics of dysfunctional families is how enmeshed they are. They are surprisingly needy. These families often spend way more time together than the average family with adult children, and expect even more. They think nothing to call you at 11 at night or even later. Whether it's in person, on the phone, text, or via email, seemingly not a day goes by without contact.

The first step then is to end that enmeshment. I just want to be clear that it's okay to be in a close relationship with someone, but it is considered unhealthy to be enmeshed with them. Enmeshment is when your life is basically not your own. You seemingly cannot do anything without your family's input. You family feels very much entitled to have a say in your life choices. You have to include them in everything. This is enmeshment and it's not healthy.

The way that you free yourself from enmeshment is you create distance.   There are a number of ways that you create distance in an enmeshed relationship. One of the core ways you do this is that you make your own decisions without informing your family first. You simply go ahead and do it and then let them find out about it afterwards. This sends a clear message that you do not need their opinions and that you are going to live your life your way from now on.

Another way to create distance is to stop being on-call. Right now, you are probably treated as an emergency on-call number. Your family calls you at any time and expects you to always pick up whether you're eating dinner, at work, or trying to sleep. They call you for all their crises, real or imagined. This needs to stop. The way you stop it is you stop answering the phone. You stop answering it at work and you turn it off after a certain hour at night. You let it go to voicemail and you only call back if they leave a voicemail message. After a while your family will realize that they can no longer use you as their on-call. If they complain about you not picking up the phone anymore, just give a two-sentence response: "I've decided to stop answering the phone after 8pm so that I can relax in the evening".

Third, when you do receive texts, emails, or voicemails, you can create distance by not responding back immediately. If it would seem sudden and dramatic for you to wait a couple hours before getting back to a family member, you can start off with just waiting ten minutes and slowly adding to the amount of time you wait. What this does is once again it communicates to your family that you are not at their beck and call. It also gives your family time to solve their problems on their own without you. It also gives them more time to think about what they want to say to you when you do get back to them rather than have a "knee jerk" or impulsive response.

You can also create distance when you ignore certain texts/voicemails/emails. Which ones you ignore depends on you. I recommend ignoring the ones that are inappropriate or make you feel uncomfortable. Some people argue that ignoring the communication is passive aggressive or immature. I disagree. It is well known in Psychology that ignoring a behavior causes it to decrease over time. So ignore the type of communications that you wish to decrease.

Lastly, we create distance when we say "no" to invites or family gatherings. If you don't want to go, say "no" rather than visit your family purely out of obligation. One of my clients had a family that expected everyone to spend their entire Sunday together, every Sunday, at the family home. This was literally half her weekend and possibly more so because it meant that all errands got pushed to Saturday. My client ended up barely getting a weekend to spend time with friends, her significant other, or just for herself. The solution was to start saying "no" and to not be overly apologetic about it either. She learned to just give a "Sorry but I made plans this weekend" and not feel bad about it. If you want to see them or it's a special event, then by all means, go and enjoy yourself. But you should also feel free to say no if you'd rather do something else with your time.

So, in summary, we create distance by:

1. Make your own decisions without informing them first
2. Stop being on-call
3. Don't respond immediately to voicemails or emails
4. Ignore emails/texts/voicemails that are inappropriate
5. Say "no" when you don't want to spend time with them

If you've employed the other strategies in this book and the relationship is still toxic, creating distance will be necessary in order to protect you from that toxicity. Creating distance is very helpful when dealing with dysfunctional people because it robs them of the instant gratification of contacting you and getting an immediate response. Without that instant gratification, their impulsive be-havior naturally decreases. The person is also able to think through their actions more and possibly solve their crises on their own rather than rely on you constantly. Even if it isn't always a crises, if they are relying on you to alleviate their boredom, that also isn't good. They need that distance in order to learn how to self-soothe and cope with uncomfortable emotions on their own.

Creating distance is also good for you because when you are so enmeshed with another person it can create conflicts in your own life. When you're absorbing so many of the emotions of another person, especially if that person is dysfunctional, those emotions can then come out in negative ways. You may find yourself feeling more irritable or more depressed. It may negatively impact the way you treat your significant other or impact your performance at work. Once you have succeeded at creating distance, you may be surprised at the ripple effect.

When to go low contact

The purpose of reducing contact is not to punish the person or make them feel bad or to try to "convince" them to be better. We can't change them. All we can do is accept that they are the way they are and to work with what we know about them. By accepting them for who they truly are, we can pick up on their patterns of behavior and use that to protect yourself. That being said, you go low contact when you've done everything else in this book and you are still encountering mistreatment.

Most of my clients find that there is some minimal amount of time spent with their family where it's okay. One of my clients, Missy, found that her visits with her family often started out okay, but then started to degrade after the third day. Like clockwork, starting the fourth day, her sister would start picking on her ("joking around") and then the rest of her family would join in. By the fifth day it was an all-out battle and they would not be on speaking terms for a month afterwards. In this case the solution was simple: strictly limit yourself to three days, no exceptions.

For my other client, Derek, spending days with his family was not an option. Even just one full or half day spent together would turn into a nightmare. For him, just spending more than one hour together was too much. It wasn't long after that hour that his family would start acting up. So for him, taking vacations together was out of the question. Having lunch or stopping by for a short visit was as much as he could handle.

Other people may find that it's not so much the amount of time spent together, but rather specific situations that need to be avoided. I want you to think about your own family for a minute here. Do they mistreat you all the time or are there specific situations where it is worse? From now on I want you to do your best to avoid the situations that you know it will be bad. One of my clients realized that for some reason Sunday afternoons was a bad time for his mother, so he learned to stop interacting with her on Sundays. For another client, it was when her mother was hosting a party. She learned to avoid her mother for the week prior and to just stop by shortly during the middle of one of her mother's parties.

Many people from dysfunctional families find that the holidays, or certain "high pressure" holidays like Christmas and Thanksgiving are the absolute worst for them. During this time, the abuse and passive aggressive behavior is at an all-time high. There are a couple of reasons for why this might be. One reason is because your family or particular family member is under a lot of stress/pressure from the holidays. They then cope with that stress by taking it out on you.

Another possible reason for why their behavior towards you is worse during the holidays is because they feel more like they can get away with it during that time. *You're not* really *going to call me out in front of Grandma, are you? You're not* really *going to walk out in the middle of Thanksgiving dinner, are you?* They may also feel that you are more of a captive audience during the holidays. *Of course you're going to come and spend the whole day with us, it's Christmas!* But actually, you don't have to spend the holidays with anyone, especially if there's a high likelihood of you being tortured during the process.

That's right, you can avoid participating in any situation where it's going to be unpleasant for you. As an adult, you are not obligated to spend your time with them. You can simply say "We've decided to spend the holidays with my in-laws this year." Remember, follow the two-sentence rule and keep it short and sweet yet assertive.

You may also find that it's not so much the time duration or situation, but rather having them all together. Many of my clients find that individually, their family members are perfectly pleasant people. It's when they all get together, or in certain combinations, that it's a nightmare.

If you think about it, it makes perfect since that they would be better individually but completely dysfunctional as a group. Just as they had you as part of an equation that equaled dysfunction, each of your family members has a part in that equation too. When you put them all together, the equation is complete and the result is toxic. Many of my clients have found that they can continue to have contact with their family so long as it is on an individual basis and then keep time spent as a group extremely limited.

Some people find that even individually their family or certain family members can still be very toxic. However, you may still able to work around this. One of the common traits of dysfunctional people is that they can do "the normal act" quite well when motivated to. One of these motivations is if there is a witness present. Perhaps your family can act quite normal when a certain neighbor stops by to visit or if you have a friend with you. If this is the case with your family, you can plan to only be in contact with them when you have such a witness with you. It takes some planning, but it can be done.

How low is low enough?

This is the question that's on everybody's mind. Just how low is low enough? It's really very hard to say. The only way to know for certain is to do some experimenting. You can start by being more mindful of the times and situations where your dysfunctional family's behavior is at its worse. It may seem like their behavior is just random, but most people do have a pattern that you can learn and then adapt to.

It's unlikely that you will be able to eliminate all negative behavior. Remember, even in "normal" families people will occasionally act negatively. You can't expect someone to be perfect; however we can expect to reduce the negativity down to a tolerable level with only the occasional upset.

It's important to also pay attention to how you feel after spending time with your family. Do you feel happy and energized or do you feel irritable, exhausted, and kind of depressed? Sometimes the manipulation and abuse can be covert enough that you can't quite put your finger on why you feel awful after spending time with them, you just know you feel bad. It's important to pay attention to these feelings because it may be a sign that abuse and/or manipulation is ongoing. If that's the case, you may want to decrease your contact further and see if that makes a difference in how you feel.

Keep experimenting until you find what works. Most people find that there is some minimal amount of contact that they are able to have that will allow them to continue to have a relationship with their family. It's important to understand that you don't have to make any kind of announcement that you are reducing contact. It's actually the stronger position to just reduce contact and not say anything to them about it. Remember, they don't have a say in how you choose to live your life.

By telling them what you're doing, it's like you're inviting them to share their opinion on the matter. You are also giving them the opportunity to debate you on the merits of your plan. Getting into a debate or argument with them is not a good idea since most likely these are not people who can listen to reason. It's far better to just go ahead with your experiment and let them figure it out later, if they ever do.

You may be surprised how much you can reduce your contact with your dysfunctional family and not have them even say anything about it. On the other hand, it also would not be uncommon for them to say something about it. In that case, it's perfectly fine to tell them that you've been busy. Everyone's busy so it's not a lie. You *are* busy and since your free time is rare and valuable, you are choosing to spend it in ways that are more enjoyable for you. So there's nothing wrong with simply telling them "I've been busy lately" and leaving it at that.

Another tactic is to ignore these inquiries. Just change the subject or not respond. Eventually you probably will have to say *something*, but you are letting them know that the way you spend your free time is not up for debate.

Conclusion

Reducing the amount of contact with your family is a very usefully strategy if your family is very enmeshed or if the other strategies used in this book have not been successful on their own. Of course, you should continue to use those other strategies as they are part of having healthy boundaries, but you may have to reduce contact as well.

Some people find that just reducing the overall contact with their family a little is enough to restore healthy interactions. Others find that they need to greatly reduce their contact with their family in order to preserve their sanity. Still others find that they are able to have a good amount of contact with their family so long as they are careful to avoid certain situations or only spend time with their family on an individual basis. The important thing is to experiment and to just see what works for you.

One of the great benefits of reducing contact is that it gives you enough distance from the problem in order to gain a new perspective. I'll give you an example: I used to have really bad stomach issues. The doctor told me that it was just because of stress or anxiety. I considered that this was a possibility, but I also felt like it had something to do with my food. There was only one way to find out, and that was to eliminate food and see what happened.

So, I fasted. I removed all food from my diet and noticed that all of my stomach issues resolved as a result of this. As it turned out, I had developed lactose intolerance. Lactose intolerance was the cause of my stomach issues, not stress and anxiety. It wasn't me that was the problem; it was dairy.

You may be going through a similar situation with your family. You may find yourself questioning still "Is it me or is it them?" Of course, they want you to believe it's you. But there's only one way to find out for certain. You have to go on your own fast from your family and see what happens. Give yourself a couple of days (or perhaps weeks) without them and see how you feel. You may be surprised the difference it makes in your life to have reduced contact.

This is the beauty of going low contact with a dysfunctional family. It gives you the space and distance to be freed from their influence. You can continue to have some contact with them, but you also have the freedom to start living your own life.

8

No Contact

Sandra suffered greatly while living with her mother. Her mother truly terrorized her, and if it wasn't her mother, it was one of her mother's boyfriend's. Sandra remembers a time that her mother pinned her down on her bed while her boyfriend beat her. For Sandra, this was like being raped and at the time, she was afraid that she would indeed be raped by the boyfriend afterwards. And why not? The message her mother was giving her was that she would never do anything to protect her.

No matter what horrific and abusive things her mother did to her, it was always Sandra's fault. Sandra was the problem child. Sandra was the one who needed to see a therapist and needed to be put on medication. At times Sandra even found herself agreeing that maybe she was the problem and maybe she did bring it upon herself.

Sandra remembers a time in her early teen years where she opened up and told a therapist about some of the things going on with her mother. The therapist asked that her mother then go with her to her next appointment so that these things could be addressed. Sure enough, at the next appointment, Sandra's mother joined them. In front of her mother, Sandra told the therapist some of the things that were going on at home. The therapist then told Sandra and her mother that if these things were true, she would have to report them.

Both the therapist and her mother then just stared at Sandra in silence. She knew that if she stuck with the truth that she would end up in a foster home and her mother may go to jail. So Sandra looked down at the floor and said monotonously "It never happened. I was lying." It should have been obvious to everyone that Sandra was lying just to avoid a report being filed, but the therapist seemed happy to go with it in order to avoid an incident. Sandra never saw the therapist again and her mother seemed happy with that, although her mother never missed an opportunity to tell someone how Sandra had "lied" to her therapist about being abused.

It was around this time that Sandra realized that she was never going to be seen in a good way, so why even bother trying? She owned her "otherness". She decided to literally wear it on her face so as to not disappoint anyone. The way Sandra did this was by becoming "Goth" in High School. She found that being Goth actually worked for her. Her new appearance attracted other abused and neglected kids at her school and they formed a supportive friendship. For a while, this seemed to make things better.

Sandra was still depressed and still miserable living with her mother. But what were her options? Go to a foster home? Kill herself? The option her mother seemed to like best was to keep Sandra over-medicated on various anti-depressants, mood stabilizers, and anxiolytics. When Sandra was 19 and in her first year of College, one night she found that taking all of these psychiatric medications had finally caught up to her. In the middle of the night, Sandra got out of bed to go to the bathroom and immediately fell to the floor. The room was spinning and she couldn't stand. She felt nauseous and dizzy.

Sandra crawled down the hallway to the bathroom and threw up in the toilet hoping that that would make her feel better, but all it did was make her feel more light-headed. She felt like she might pass out. That's when Sandra panicked and seriously became afraid that she might pass out and then never wake up. Her mother's bedroom was right next to the bathroom so she pounded on the door. Her mother came to the door and had an enraged look on her face. "What?!" she demanded.

Sandra was lying on the floor in front of her door with vomit on her face. She must have been a terrible sight to see. "I need you to call an ambulance" Sandra pleaded. Her mother just slammed her bedroom door and locked it. It was clear to Sandra she was on her own. The phone was attached to the wall in the highway and she couldn't reach it without standing. She tried repeatedly to crawl up the wall until she was finally able to knock the phone free and call 911.

Her mother didn't leave her bedroom until the EMTs were in the hallway outside her bedroom, lifting Sandra into a stretcher. Her mother tried to play the supportive role and asked to ride in the ambulance but Sandra refused to let her. Sandra then spent the whole night and much of the morning at the hospital getting well. She then took a bus home and packed a bag.

That moment where her mother couldn't even be bothered to call 911 to save her life was a defining moment for Sandra. It was then that she cut off all contact with her mother. She moved away, she got off all her medications and stopped being Goth. She discovered her own style, finished College, and met a wonderful man and got married. She was living a wonder life without her mother. She hadn't felt depressed in years.

She and her husband Steve had a beautiful baby girl together. After having a daughter of her own, Sandra started to question things. Was her mother really that bad or was she just misremembering what had happened? Back then she was a teen-ager after all. Teenagers are difficult, so maybe she was partly to blame too. When she told Steve stories about her mother, she wondered if he really believed her. Some of it was hard to believe, even for her. Maybe she was wrong about what really happened.

As they were planning her daughter's first birthday, people started asking her if she was going to invite her mother. Steve thought she should. He thought it was important that their daughter know her grandmother. It's been so many years, even if she really was bad back then, maybe she's changed? Besides, she wouldn't act up in front of her granddaughter. With all this in mind, Sandra mailed her mother an invitation to the birthday party.

Everyone was at the party, including her mother. At first it seemed pleasant enough. Her mother seemed to be mingling and making an effort to get along with Sandra's friends and in-laws.

Then Sandra realized what was happening. Her mother was regaling them with tales from her teenage years. All those things that Sandra would rather have forgotten were being told to her in-laws. Her mother told them how Sandra used to be Goth, how Sandra "lied" about being abused to a therapist, how Sandra "overdosed on her medication for attention".

Sandra called her mother into the kitchen so they could speak in private. Sandra said assertively to her mother "I'd appreciate if you would refrain from telling embarrassing stories about me. I have plenty of stories I could tell them about you but I refrain from doing so out of respect for both of us." Sandra's mother then showed that same enraged face she had showed her the night that she went to the hospital. She lunged at Sandra, but Sandra ran out of the house and back to where the party was, hoping that her mother would control herself if there was a crowd of witnesses.

This did not deter Sandra's mother. She flipped over the card table that held the yet uncut birthday cake and lunged at Sandra again, this time punching her in the face. Sandra fell to the ground. Steve grabbed Sandra's mother and held her back. It took Steve plus his father and brother to drag Sandra's mother from the party. Looking back, Sandra knew she should have just called the police and filed a restraining order against her mother but at the time she felt horribly embarrassed and just wanted her mother out of there.

If there was ever a doubt in her mind that she could have a relationship with her mother, it was now gone. She knew once and for all that her mother was incapable of change. She was who she was, and Sandra needed to accept that. She never contacted her mother again. One of the fortunate things about having this incident take place in front of everyone Sandra knew was that now they all knew why Sandra didn't want to have contact with her mother and they never pressured her again.

Most people find that there is some minimal amount of contact that they can have with their family, even if it's just spending Christmas with them once a year. However, some people find, like Sandra did, that they cannot have any contact with them at all.

Going "no contact" means that you have completely cut off your family or specific family members. You have zero contact with them moving forward. You don't even send them a birthday card or respond to their emails. To do so otherwise would mean to be very low contact, as opposed to no contact. As an intelligence agent would say, you go completely dark.

This is obviously very controversial. As Sandra found, other people were initially not willing to accept that she would completely cut off her own mother. For people that grew up in functional families, this sounds cruel or even petty. They just can't understand why it would ever be necessary to completely cut off a family member.

Society as a whole is also very much against the dissolution of a family. We are told to "honor thy father and thy mother". Indeed, governments and civilizations seem to depend on stable families in order to hold society together. It is for this reason that they do everything in their power to discourage people from cutting off family members.

For the most part, this is a good thing. When a family is functional, it is perhaps the most blessed thing in existence. When a family is dysfunctional, it only harms those still caught within it. If you are able to have some contact with your family without enduring abuse, then it is perhaps best to preserve that contact. However, there are instances where it is necessary to not have any contact at all.

One of those instances is when the person is simply incapable of change or of controlling themselves. This may be due to the person's untreated mental illness, or due to drug use. In the case of Sandra's mother, one thing we know for certain is that her behavior is not normal. Her bizarre behavior could be easily attributeed to untreated mental illness, such as narcissistic personality disorder, or by a hidden drug addiction that Sandra did not know about.

In Sandra's case, her mother certainly fits the criteria for no contact. To begin with, there was already a history of emotional and physical abuse. Then, even after years of having no contact with her daughter she couldn't control herself for her granddaughter's first birthday party. When dealing with someone that abusive and out of control, having contact isn't an option.

Avoiding a power struggle

If you do decide to end contact with your family or certain family members, it is wise to try to avoid getting into a power struggle with your family over it. A power struggle is when you and your family get into a tug-of-war for power and control.

In a lot of ways, the temptation to get into a power struggle with your family is understandable. After spending so long under their thumb and not having any personal control in your life, you can be left with a strong desire to take their power away from them. One of the ways that people engage in power struggles is by giving ultimatums: "Either play according to my rules, or else!"

Although it's understandable that you would have a desire to do this, I'm still going to advise you not to do it. The reason for this is that your family doesn't fight fair. If you get into a power struggle with them, they will take the conflict to levels that you are not prepared to go. This is not a battle you can win. Remember, the only way to win is to not play the game.

It is due to this, that you should never use cutting off contact as a threat or ultimatum. You should also never use it as a way to punish someone or try to coerce their behavior. Some of my clients have told me that they want to cut off contact to show their family that they are serious and that they need to change or else risk losing them. You really don't want to play that game as your family has ways of getting back at you. Don't cut off contact with your family unless you are serious about it.

In addition, I would advise against making any official announcement that you are going no-contact. There are several reasons for why you would not want to do this. For one, your family will find this to be extremely provocative. No matter how carefully you craft this announcement, it will most likely be seen by your family as a declaration of war. Your family member may feel especially enraged at the embarrassment and humiliation of you ending your relationship with them in such a public way.

This is also another instance where informing your family of your decisions makes them feel that they have a say in it. If you're going no-contact, you really don't have to say anything. You simply stop contacting them and ignore their attempts to have a correspondence with you. By doing it this way, you are instead giving the message that this is not up for debate and that it is pointless for them to try to change your mind.

Thirdly, you don't want to make any kind of announcement because you may one day change your mind. No matter how certain you may be in the moment that you will never have any contact with your family ever again, the fact is that it is possible that you may one day change your mind. The truth is, most attempts to go no-contact do not last forever. In fact, most last for less than a year. You want to leave the door open so that you can go back if you ever decide you want to.

Lastly, making an announcement all but guarantees the involvement of the rest of your family. You want to keep your family and extended family out of this as much as possible. This is just between you and the individual or individuals you are ending contact with. Even if you think the rest of your family doesn't like this particular family member either, you may find that they still dislike the idea of you cutting off this person.

That being said, it's better to let things "fizzle out" as opposed to have a dramatic end to the relationship. Hopefully you have first tried having minimal contact with the person and creating distance. It may be better to just keep minimizing contact until there is no contact. Families are often more accepting of this type of dissolution and the person in particular you are cutting off can then save face by claiming that perhaps the ending of the relationship was more mutual. In general, the more they are able to save face, the less drama and retaliation there will be.

What you can expect the first year

The first year you go no-contact is the hardest. Often the decision to go no-contact is trigger by a "final straw" event; one last argument or incident of mistreatment where you decide that you simply can't take it any longer. So you stop contacting your family and wait for the fall-out to happen.

Sometimes the fall-out is simply that you no longer have contact anymore, but other times the person in particular starts seeking out allies to help defend them against what they perceive as an attack against them. These allies are typically other people in the family. Even if this particular person causes lots of problems for everyone else, don't be surprised if your other family members still defend them.

Some people feel a great need to "preserve the family". They may worry that by having you cut off one person in the family that they may be next to go, so for their own sense of security and safety, they want you to take back the disowned family member. They may also feel resentment that you no longer have to deal with it while they still have to because they lack the courage to go no-contact as well.

The best way to deal with these "allies" is to just say something like "I don't hate mom, I'm not angry, I wish her the best in life, but I've found that we just can't spend time together without there being a conflict. This is something I need to do in order to have healthy boundaries and I hope that you can respect that." Don't try to put the blame on the ousted family member. It isn't about blame, it's about heaving boundaries.

Remember, you want to be above the fray. By staying calm and assertive, you are telling the rest of your family more than you ever could be giving a long explanation or getting into a debate with them. While they're listening to the disowned family member bad-mouth you, they will think about how you were able to keep your cool and you will be perceived as the better person. However, it may be a good idea to have less contact and create distance with these "allies" if you feel that they trying to provoke you or are fishing for information to give to the ousted family member.

Something you have to be prepared for is the possibility that your family will side with the other family member permanently. It's not uncommon for them to present you with an ultimatum of their own: "Either have a relationship with all of us or none of us". One of my clients found that when she went no-contact with a destructive narcissistic family member that the rest of her family disowned her. Of course, you have to ask yourself if you still want to have contact with the rest of them when they show so little consideration for your feelings.

Another consequence the first year of going no-contact is that you may enter into a period of mourning. Just like how you would mourn the death of a family member, many people find that they mourn the loss of the relationship when they go no-contact. You may even find yourself reverting back to an almost child-like state where it takes everything in you not to yell "Please don't be mad at me, mommy!"

Often times, it's not even the actual relationship you're mourning, but rather mourning the way the relationship could have been. By going no-contact, you're giving up the hope that they will ever change or get better, and emotionally that's very painful. You probably still wish you could have a normal parent-child or sibling relationship with the person. Now you have to give up that dream.

The good news is that most people find that it gets easier after the first year. By the end of the first year, your relationship has reached its conclusion one way or another. By now the people in your life have accepted that you won't be having a relationship with that person. You may have lost a few more people along the way, but the matter is at least resolved now and it is unlikely that there will be more drama.

You may find that after the first year you hardly ever think of the person that you cut off. People have described it as a sort of emotional divorce. Intellectually, you know that this person is your sister (or brother, or parent, etc) but emotionally they just feel like a regular person; some stranger that you hear of occasionally. When people ask you if you have any siblings, you may find that you forget to even mention them. It's like they're no longer your family. The familial attachment has been severed and they no longer have any power to hurt you.

Restoring contact

Most people find that they are unable to maintain no-contact for the entire year. Three months seems to be the average length of time before people pursue contact again. There are various reasons for why a person would restore contact. The parent-child bond is very strong and it is difficult to sever. Going no-contact with a sibling or other extended relative is probably easier than ending contact with a parent completely. People who do not miss their relative after going no-contact are also more likely to be able to maintain silence. Those experiencing a lot of negative emotions after ending contact are more likely to resume contact.

The important thing to remember is that restoring contact doesn't mean that you are a failure. Probably most people end up going through several phases of no-contact before they are able to end it for good. But it's also important to remember that "ending it for good" may not be necessary for all people. If you miss your family and you think that you can make it work, then perhaps it's better to restore contact. Only you know what's best for you.

I remember my client Stephanie. She hadn't had contact with her father for five years. She wasn't alone in her decision to go no-contact either. All of her father's children had no-contact with him. Her father had gone through several marriages. Each of his children had been a product of one of these failed marriages. He seemed to leave a path of destruction and broken homes every-where he went.

There was no "event" that triggered Stephanie ending contact with her father. As she became an adult, she simply saw him less and less until she stopped seeing him completely. She got tired of hearing his criticism of her when he himself had made the worst life choices of anyone she knew. By the time she stopped talking to her father, all of her older siblings had already cut him off, so her father didn't bother trying to fight for the relationship. He let her go as well.

When Stephanie ended contact with her father, she didn't feel bad about it. There was no guilt or remorse. She didn't miss him at all. She already had a great relationship with her mother and siblings and didn't feel a need to include him in that. For the first five years of her separation from her father, Stephanie was perfectly fine.

Then something changed for Stephanie at the fifth year of no-contact. One of her close friends' fathers died and she saw how grief-stricken her friend was. It then dawned on her that no-contact meant that her father could die while they were not on good terms. She decided that she couldn't live with that. Stephanie decided to reach out to her father.

After five years of no-contact, Stephanie felt anxious about initiating contact. She was afraid that her father would be angry with her or unwelcoming. She was afraid that he would lecture her about not talking to him for so long. Fortunately, the reality was not at all had she had feared. Her father was welcoming, grateful to be hearing from her, and did not bring up the long period of silence between them. They were able to pick up where they had left off.

Stephanie found that her father was different now. He was three years sober and had steady employment. He was not perfect. He was still a dysfunctional person, but he kept his dysfunction to himself rather than drag Stephanie into it. Stephanie found that she was now able to have a relationship with her father, and she was glad that she had had the courage to reach out to him.

It's okay to leave the door open for restoring contact. You may find that with time and distance, your family learns that they simply must respect your boundaries. Going no-contact is part of maintaining boundaries. Remember, you can't say you have boundaries if you don't enforce them. The ultimate enforcement of boundaries is to end contact with someone who repeatedly violates them. For some people, this is the only way that they learn that they must change their behavior.

Stephanie's father didn't realize his behavior was a problem until he had had four failed marriages and no family that would talk to him anymore. It sounds extreme, but some people need those kinds of behavioral consequences before they will realize that they need to change. In Stephanie's case, her father did change and she was able to have a relationship with him again. This is something that sometimes happens and you should be open to this possibility, although I don't think you should bank on it either.

Giving up the hope for understanding

Part of going no-contact is giving up the hope that your family will ever understand what they have done to you. This is probably the hardest thing for people. Once you realize that you are in fact not the "bad one" or the "crazy one", it's natural to have a strong desire to make your family realize that as well. The thing you need to understand though is that if they can't realize that they abused you on their own, then there's nothing you can do to make them have that realization.

I am fully aware of when I have mistreated someone, and I feel bad about it afterwards. I feel remorseful. I even feel bad about little things, like not holding the door open for someone or accidentally cutting them in line. Even though the vast majority of the bad things I do are unintentional, I still feel very sorry about it.

It would not be necessary for a friend or family member to send me a multi-page email trying to explain to me how I've hurt them because I would have already sent my own email apologizing for what had happened. And if someone did send me such an email about how I had caused harm to them without realizing it, I would have been horrified that they would be so hurt and wouldn't be able to apologize enough. I wouldn't argue with the person about how what I did was unintentional and therefor they have no right to be hurt and that second-of-all they are hurting me by sending this email. I would instead be focusing on repairing the relationship.

That is how a person capable of empathy and self-awareness responds to hurting another person. If your family was capable of this kind of understanding, they would have already showed it by now. It should not be such a struggle to have some-one understand that they've hurt you, especially when you consider some of the outrageous and blatantly abusive things they have done to you. If they don't know what they've done already, it's unlikely that they will ever understand.

You will not be able to win a debate with them or write a multi-page email convincing enough that they will feel empathy for what they have done to you. You've probably already tried this approach and seen that it doesn't work. If you've never confronted them, then perhaps it's worth a try, but don't get your hopes up. You know what the truth is, and that's all that matters.

This is probably the most frustrating part of all of it; having to accept that you will never get that recognition from your family. Your family or particular family member maintains that they are completely blameless and it's everybody else's fault, or mostly just your fault. A question that I get often is "How can they believe that they are completely blameless? Do they really believe that or is it just an act?" Well, we can't read their minds, so no one knows for sure, but perhaps I can shed some light on the situation.

As a therapist, I've been blessed to have a wide variety of clientele. Some of my clients have included narcissists. Now, no one goes into therapy saying "I need help for my narcissism". Typically they come in because they are having problems with absolutely everyone in their life (family, neighbors, co-workers) and want to vent to a therapist about it. What gives them away is that they claim to be 100% blameless in every situation. As a therapist, I recognize that sometimes people are blameless and that some people do get targeted, but you have to ask yourself if it's possible for this to be the case every time.

What I have discovered is that the narcissist is very confused by other people. They think that they are just being personable and charming and can't understand why other people are so put-off by their personality. Rather than try to adjust their approach, they decide that they are right and other people are wrong and that these other people are unfairly persecuting them. They also don't see anything wrong with seeking revenge for this unfair persecution and see this as "fair play". They wreak havoc in their own lives and don't see that they are the ones doing it.

I've found that trying to help them see that what they are doing is wrong doesn't work. That's usually when they fire me as their therapist. So I'd rather that they just change their behavior even without gaining the insight. Now I take the approach, "Whether you're to blame or not, this isn't working for you. Would you like to learn better ways of responding that will work for you?" Some get better but some don't. But, even the ones that get better don't seem to ever understand the ways that they hurt other people. To them, it's always everyone else.

A lot of people have a hard time believing that someone could have so little insight as to always think it's everyone else, but I do think it's possible. I actually had a similar experience myself. During a flight landing, my ears popped so hard that my left ear hurt really badly. My ear hurt for three days but then the pain went away and when the pain dissipated I assumed it meant that there was no longer anything wrong with my ear. I've always had excellent hearing and I assumed I still did.

After the plane incident, my husband kept scolding me for "talking too loud". I thought he was just picking on me and I would get mad and say "I'm talking normal. You're the one who's talking so softly that I can barely hear you!" I started getting really annoyed at how quiet everyone would talk. People were talking so softly that I had to strain to hear them and was missing pieces of the conversation.   I felt frustrated and irritated about it much of the time.

When I went to the doctor for my yearly check-up, the doctor looked in my ears and told me that there was a puncture in my left ear drum. I then realized that it was me, not everyone else. Yes, rather than just figure out that there was something wrong with my hearing, I instead thought that the entire world had gotten quieter. Why would I make such a huge error in thinking? I think that part of it is that there is a lot of shame involved in losing your hearing. I would have never thought it was a shameful thing prior to losing my own hearing, but when it happened to me I felt really embarrassed about it. I also found that people get oddly defensive and give you strange looks when you say "I'm sorry but could you speak louder? I'm having a hard time hearing you." I didn't want other people to know. I think I also didn't want to admit to myself that this was happening to me at such a young age as well. I think a similar process happens to narcissists.

Obviously it's not popular to be a narcissist and it's not something that anyone would wish for themselves. I think that perhaps part of them knows that they are this way, but it's too distressing to fully admit to yourself that there is something deeply wrong with who you are. It's thus easier to tell yourself that it's everyone else who is wrong or to say "This is just how the world works. Everyone uses other people; I'm just good at it and thus entitled to do these things".

You have to accept that your family member has spun such a web of rationalization that if they can't see it for themselves, that there's nothing you can do to break through it. As I've said, even therapists find it difficult if not impossible to get through to them. I also wonder if underneath the self-righteous façade there's so much guilt and shame that they are afraid that if they were to ever tap into it that the pain would be so unbearable that it would destroy them. I certainly don't envy them, and I know that this isn't a popular thing to say, but I feel a lot of sympathy for the distress that they have in their lives.

I don't want anyone to be afraid to fly on an airplane because of what happened to my hearing, so I want you to know that I am not 100% certain that the flight is what caused the puncture in my ear drum. It seems to be what caused it, but who knows. Also, the puncture has since healed and my hearing is back to normal now. I've flown plenty of times since the ear-popping incident, so I haven't let it hold me back from traveling and neither should you. I wouldn't want my experience to rob you of the fun of traveling.

Conclusion

Completely ending contact with a family member is not a decision to be taken lightly. Typically it is only done because you have no other choice: the person won't respect your boundaries and seems incapable of self-control. Going no-contact is not done as a way to "punish" a person either. No-contact is also not to be done in order to try to coerce someone into changing. At best that would be manipulation and at worse it would be emotional abuse. Only do it if you are truly prepared to end the relationship.

Before making the decision to go no-contact, you should be prepared for any possible consequences. It is not unusual for the ousted family member to go on the "war path" once they realize that you are serious. It is also not unusual for them to seek out other family members to help them wage war against you. Some have found that going no-contact with one family member means having to go no-contact with all of them.

Even if the family does not turn against you, most find that the first year of no-contact is very difficult. It's not unlike mourning the death of a family member. It is a sort of death, as you go through the process of severing the emotional bonds between you. Seeing a therapist during this time can be very helpful.

I want to remind you though that you don't have to be no-contact forever. Probably for most people, the period of no-contact between them and family is only temporary. Some people do have the ability to change or to at least control themselves better when they are in your presence. Some people also find that the time without their family is a time of personal reflection. During this period of silence, most people find that they gain a new perspective about their family. You may find that through this gained insight that you can develop a strategy that allows you to have contact with them without being abused.

Part 3

Forging your own path

9

Taking your life back

Although Carlo was an only child, he grew up in a large family. He had lots of Aunts and Uncles and lots of cousins. They all lived together in the same town and everyone would get together frequently even though nobody seemed to get along. There was always some "drama" in the family. From a young age, Carlo got used to the sight of adults crying at the dinner table and the door slamming as someone stormed out.

Carlo always felt like a disappointment to his family. His parents had wanted to have lots of children, but his mother was only able to produce him after suffering from several miscarriages. Carlo felt that he was far from being their "dream child". Starting from first grade he was put in Special Ed. He had dyslexia which not only kept him from succeeding at reading and writing, it also hurt his ability to do math because the numbers would appear to be switched around.

Carlo knew his father was deeply ashamed of Carlo being in Special Ed. His father would force him to sit at the dinner table and study for hours and hours. Meanwhile, his cousin Anthony was excelling academically. Carlo knew that Anthony was the real star of the family. He was smart, handsome, and witty, whereas Carlo felt that he was neither of those things. He was compared to

Anthony constantly and told that he needed to try harder and to use Anthony as a role model.

Carlo finally did fight his way out of Special Ed. He learned tricks so that his dyslexia wasn't such a problem and studied long hours so that he could get his grades up. Carlo kept getting A's so finally the school moved him to a normal class.

Carlo at first felt really proud of himself. After all, most Special Ed. Students stayed in Special Ed. their whole time in school. Very few ever made it to a normal classroom and Carlo knew how hard he had worked to make it happen. However, Carlo's family did not celebrate with him and really did not even acknowledge it. To them, being in a normal classroom was just expected, so they were not going to praise something that was to them just normal. They made it clear to Carlo that he was going to have to do much better if they were going to acknowledge him.

Carlo continued to work really hard in school. By his Senior year of High School he was in all Honors classes. However, he was once again not given the acknowledgement he craved. Anthony was still the star. Anthony was the class President and the one who made everyone proud.

Carlo's grandmother had set up a college fund for her grandchildren. She used it to pay for Anthony to get a Liberal Arts degree at a private University. Carlo did not receive any money for College. He instead chose to work and take a few classes at the local Community College. A couple years after Anthony graduated; his grandmother gave him $50,000 so that Anthony could start a fence installing business. Carlo didn't feel entitled to his grand-mother's money, but he still felt hurt that he was repeatedly passed-over when he felt that he too could have gone to a good school or started his own business if given the money.

Carlo was pressured by his family into working for Anthony's business. He finally agreed and did things like data-entry, billing, and other administrative tasks. The business seemed to be doing alright. Carlo didn't get a great salary, but he was always good at not spending more than he had to and managed to accumulate a decent Savings. Meanwhile, Anthony seemed to be spending money with abandon. He drove a flashy car and just bought a big house. Of course, the rest of the family loved that Anthony was doing this. He continued to be in the spotlight while Carlo stayed in the shadows.

As it turned out, Anthony had not been paying his taxes for a number of years. When he was audited, he just narrowly avoided being sent to jail. The business was shut down and all of the employees were laid-off, including Carlo. The reaction of his family surprised Carlo. All he heard was "Poor Anthony! The mean Government closed his business!" Carlo had certainly never gotten any sympathy or understanding for his plights and in his opinion Anthony was a criminal not deserving of sympathy. He was starting to realize that it really didn't matter what he or Anthony did. Anthony would always be the Golden Child and he would always be the disappointment.

Although most people are sad to be laid-off, for Carlo it was a blessing. He hated working for his cousin and saw this as an opportunity to do something he always wanted. He cashed out his life savings and bought film equipment. He was going to have his own film crew. This was a dream of his and he realized that it was now or never.

When Carlo told his family about his plans, they were against it. They expressed doubt that he could be successful and told him that he was being foolish. Carlo persisted and it actually wasn't long until he was filming clips and segments for the local News. It was just a couple years in and he was making more money that he ever did working for his cousin. He was living his dream and he was ecstatic.

Although Carlo was living his dream and making good money, he found that his family simply couldn't be happy for him. He was tired of hearing about Anthony. He was tired of the criticism. Carlo moved to the big city and decided that he was not going to go home for the holidays anymore. He just didn't see the point of spending his free time with people whom were so negative towards him. That year he spent a blissful Thanksgiving aboard a cruise ship and didn't regret a thing.

One of the most difficult things about taking your life back from your dysfunctional family is that at first it may seem like you are left with nothing. If you have an especially enmeshed family, it can feel like you have nothing that is truly "yours". But you do have a life! You actually have a great life; it's just been buried under dysfunction for so long that you may have forgotten what it looks like.

Like Carlo, you may find the holidays to be especially difficult. It is not unusual for the holidays to be especially difficult in toxic families and there are a number of possible reasons for why this might be. One possible reason is that the holidays are just stressful for everyone. There is a lot of pressure for everything to be "perfect" and your family is not immune to this pressure. And actually, if you do have a dysfunctional family, they probably don't handle stress well. One of the ways that they handle this stress is probably by taking it out on you, so this all comes together to create an especially unpleasant visit for you.

Another reason for the holidays being difficult is because that is one of the times that the whole family is together. We've discussed in previous chapters how sometimes dysfunctional family members can be fine individually, but when you put them all together it's Hell. And when you add extended family to the mix, you may find that there are now even more conflicts than usual. Lastly, you may find that the family acts up more than usual simply because it's "the holidays" and they feel that gives them a free pass to act however they please. They know that you will be less likely to call them out on their inappropriate behavior simply because it's the holidays and you don't want to be blamed for "ruining Thanksgiving".

Regardless of why they do it, most people in dysfunctional families find that the toxicity is brought to new levels when the holidays arrive. You may have come to dread these holidays but don't know what else to do. After all, it is the holidays and you're supposed to spend them with your family, right? But what if that's not necessarily the case? What if that's not really what the holidays are actually about?

Let's take a moment to examine why we even have holidays in the first place. Holidays were probably created sometime around the agricultural revolution. Farming required careful planning or else people would starve. If you planted your seeds too early or too late, you would ruin your crops. There was a specific time period that needed to be followed and holidays marked this time period. For the most part, they still do. Here in Boston, I plant all of my Fall bulbs before Halloween and I start planting my spring bulbs after Easter. There are probably similar holiday planting schedules where you live.

But holidays not only served as a reminder so people knew when to reap and when to sow, they also served as much needed leisure time. Farming, especially back then, is really hard work. People would toil day in and day out and holidays provided one of the few excuses for relaxation. Holidays served as a much needed break from the daily toil.

As you can see, the original purpose of holidays was to give people a break. Family really is not a part of it unless you enjoy spending time with your family. If spending time with your family during the holidays just leaves you feeling drained afterwards, then it really is not in the spirit of the holidays to be seeing them at that time. You work hard and you deserve a break too. The holidays are meant to be enjoyed, not endured.

Many of my clients initially wonder what they will do with their holidays if not spend it with their families. They imagine themselves home alone watching TV. That certainly sounds lonely and depressing and is not in the spirit of the holidays either. To give you an idea of what you can do with the holidays instead, I've decided to list out some ideas for you.

This list is mostly just Christian and American holidays and I understand that there are other holidays out there; however these are the holidays that I am familiar with. Even if these are not holidays that you celebrate, perhaps they can give you an idea of ways that you can change the ones that you have traditionally spent with your own family. The idea here is just to give some ideas to get you started. It is certainly not a prescription of how you must spend your holidays.

Also, if you are at a point in your life where you have your own family, one option is to simply take the holiday traditions you love and just do those things with your spouse and children rather than always driving to a relative's place. If there is conflict with extended family, your children would probably be happier just spending the holidays with mom and dad anyway.

Christmas

I'm going to start with Christmas since for most people this is typically the "big one". It's the holiday with the most pressure for everything to be perfect and is the one where you are dealing with the most relatives at one time. For my client Jenny, Christmas was never any fun. When she was a child, her parents would fight about the amount of money they spent on presents and it was always a tense time.

Jenny came from a large family. She was the youngest of five and had many aunts and uncles and cousins. Just as she entered adulthood, the family came up with a new rule that they would only buy presents for the children since there were just too many of them to buy gifts for everyone. The only problem was that all of Jenny's siblings had children but she didn't. Not only that, but Jenny had doubts that she ever wanted to have children at all.

Every Christmas she would go to her mother's house with a car full of gifts, watch the children unwrap them all, have an uncomfortable Christmas dinner where her mother and brother would say rude things to her, and then go home empty handed. Jenny hadn't gotten a Christmas gift from her family in years and furthermore, the children really didn't show any appreciation. She doubted that the kids even remembered which relative had given them what.

For Jenny, Christmas was just a time of year where she used up her vacation time and money. She often felt bad about the experience for weeks or more afterwards. At one point, Jenny realized that she spent enough money on Christmas to pay for a cruise. I suggested that Jenny just go on a cruise instead. At first Jenny was really skeptical of this, and then she realized that there were other family members that skipped Christmas in favor of doing their own thing. It would not be the end of the world if she had fun instead. The kids wouldn't notice that they received one less toy. Jenny decided to do it and afterwards decided to make it a new yearly tradition.

Yes, there actually are "Christmas Cruises" that cater to people just like you. You can spend the holidays sipping cocktails on the beach and hopping from island to island. For a lot of people, because their family lives far away, they end up spending so much money on going back home for Christmas that it uses up their vacation budget. If going home for the holidays is not something that you enjoy, why not use that money to take a real vacation? I have found that for some destinations, Christmas is considered off-season and it's actually a much cheaper time to visit. Depending on your family, traveling may also give you a more "legitimate" excuse to not be there.

Another option is to stay home but to have a Christmas get together with your friends. A fun idea for a Christmas party with friends is to have a "Thrift Store Christmas". Instead of spending a lot of money on gifts, people pick out an item at the thrift store. If you haven't been to a thrift store recently, you can actually get really cool vintage/antique finds for around $5. You can then do a Yankee-Swap or Secret-Santa gift exchange.

Another idea for a Christmas get-together with friends is to have what I call "Re-Giftmass". This is probably one that you would hold shortly after Christmas, perhaps even on Boxing Day. Something that my clients often complain about are the thoughtless gifts that they receive from their toxic family when their family does bother to give them gifts. Even if you don't have a toxic family, just about everyone receives gifts that just aren't in their taste. Instead of tossing those gifts in the basement or closet, why not re-gift them to someone that might actually like it?

The way re-giftmass works is everyone shows up with at least one gift they really don't want. If you have several, you can bring more. Then you can either do a yankee-swap or just let people choose from the pile if they see something they like. With all of your friends pooling together, the odds are good that everyone will be able to leave with something they like. The leftover gifts could then get donated to Good Will.

Another option is to take a special Christmas hike. If you enjoy hiking, this is a great option because hiking locations are one of the few places open on Christmas day. It is also unlikely to be crowds of people and you may find you have the woods all to yourself! My husband and I have recently discovered winter hiking and actually prefer it to summer hiking. You'll find that there are no crowds, no bugs, and you are very likely to see wildlife during your hike. I don't recommend going after a snowstorm though unless you have snow-shoes or skis because the trail won't be clear. If your experience of Christmas has been mostly one of drama, fighting, and conflict, then you'll find that going on a Christmas hike is a much more peaceful and relaxing way to experience the holiday.

These are just my ideas, but really there are endless ways that you can celebrate Christmas. Is there something that you and your friends are really in to? Why not turn that thing into a themed Christmas party? Is there something special that you've really wanted to do but can't because you typically spend your money on Christmas gifts for your unappreciative family? Now you can spend that gift money on yourself and have an experience of a lifetime every season.

Does this all just sound really selfish? It's actually not selfish because you will not be expecting any gifts from them either. They can then take that money that they would have spent on you and spend it on themselves or however they please. It's the courteous thing to do to let your family know well in advance that you will not be doing a gift exchange this year so to please not get you anything.

I would recommend letting people know sometime before Thanksgiving since some people start shopping early. Although people are resistant to no longer doing the gift-exchange at first, you may be surprised to find that many of your family members decide to do the same thing.

Thanksgiving

Thanksgiving is also a holiday that people often have difficulty with. Even in not-so-toxic families, there is often a lot of pressure to have everything be perfect, everyone is together, and there are lots and lots of work. The times that I've hosted Thanksgiving dinner, it meant getting up early and cooking for 6-8 hours. The day before was also spent doing an extra good-cleaning of the house and polishing silver. After all of that work, to hear complaining from family is very hard to take.

For a lot of people, Thanksgiving dinner is a lot of work and a lot of stress simply to keep a tradition going. But perhaps if we take a closer look at the history of the holiday, we can come up with activities that are more enjoyable but still are in keeping with the meaning of the holiday. In 1620, the colonists arrived at Plymouth harbor sometime around November. They had hoped to arrive in the Spring but were delayed. They were now facing a harsh and long New England winter with very little supplies.

That first winter was very hard on the settlers that we would later refer to as "the Pilgrims". Most of them were already outcasts of society and most had left their families behind. Perhaps you can relate to them? They were trying to create a new life for themselves, but sadly, about half of them died that first winter.

When Spring finally came, there were still problems. They found farming and planting to be difficult, but they finally got the hang of it thanks to the natives who helped them and taught them. That first harvest must have been glorious. They must have been truly grateful for that food because if they had not been able to master agriculture that season, it is very likely that the rest of them would have died by the following winter. They were grateful for the harvest, grateful to be alive, and grateful for their friends.

That first Thanksgiving, they were not surrounded by family. Their family had either died that first winter or been left behind in England. Rather, they were surrounded by their friends. These were the people whom had helped them survive and this included the local natives. The first Thanksgiving was a celebration of survival and friendship. "Family" really had nothing to do with it.

Therefore, it is actually more in keeping with the spirit of Thanksgiving to celebrate it with friends and with the people whom have helped you that year. One of my clients introduced me to something called "Friendsgiving" which I think is perfect for this. The way Friendsgiving works is that you invite a bunch of friends over either on Thanksgiving or the weekend before. Everyone brings a signature dish with them and shares it with everyone. Not only is this a really good time, but no one person is responsible for doing all of the cooking. It is just like the original Thanksgiving.

What if you just want to have a good meal but don't want all of the pressure of cooking and cleaning and entertaining? Yes, there are options for you! Many hotels and fancy restaurants host special Thanksgiving dinners. All you have to do is make your reservation, show up, and sit back. I've noticed that the options for this seem to be getting better every year as some venues are also including entertainment with the meal.

Maybe big extravagant dinners aren't your thing. Something that a lot of people do on Thanksgiving is attend a football game. You can go see a football game at your local High School or College. I actually prefer going to a High School or College game over a professional game because there is often a lot more heart and spirit with the amateur players. The fans are also more fun. If you like football, this will be a great new tradition for you.

Another common way of celebrating Thanksgiving that you may have never heard of is that a lot of people actually go to the movies on Thanksgiving. Yes, a lot of movie theaters are open because this is something a lot of people like to do. If you want to make it extra special, some theaters have a special "luxury section" where you get big seats and a dinner with your movie. I recommend doing that if you have one of those special theaters near where you live.

Another idea is to do some charity work on Thanksgiving. Typically people think of serving food in a soup kitchen or homeless shelter, but there are other options. If you enjoy shopping and enjoy the madness that is Black Friday, you can shop for gifts for needy children. There are also a number of charity races that take place on Thanksgiving. If interacting with strangers seems too scary or awkward, you can even just pick up trash at a local park. If you are willing to volunteer your time, there are a lot of Thanksgiving day opportunities out there for you.

Mother's Day & Father's Day

Many of my clients have complained to me that even though they have their own children, Mother's Day and Father's Day is still entirely about their own parents and not them. If this is the case for you, I want you to take a moment to think about something. When you were a child, was Mother's Day about your grandmother or was it about your mother? If it was about celebrating your mother, then that means that your mother has been being celebrated for two generations and that's not fair. It's your turn now.

Mother's Day and Father's Day is not about grandparents. Grandparent's Day is celebrated on the first Sunday after Labor Day. Now it's time for you to have your moment of appreciation for all that you do for your family. Talk to your spouse/partner about creating a new tradition. It could be the standard activities such as a brunch, garden stroll, fishing trip, etc. Or you can do something unique and totally up to you. But either way, it is important that your children at least have one day devoted to expressing their appreciation for all that you do.

Does this mean that you should completely ignore your own parents on Mother's Day or Father's Day? Unless you are no-contact with your parents I would not recommend doing this. It would probably be a good idea to mail them a card or small gift in order to avoid hurt feelings and family drama. But remember, the day itself should be about you and your children.

What if you don't have any contact with your parents and don't have any children of your own? Something that a friend of mine does is she has renamed Mother's Day as "Wife Appreciation Day". You can of course also have a "Husband Appreciation Day" Father's Day too! On Mother's Day she does all the fun stuff that people usually do for their mothers, but instead her husband does these things for her. Rather than feel sad about their lack of relationship with their parents, they instead celebrate their marriage.

Mother's Day doesn't have to be all about lavish celebrations if that's not your thing. Something I've noticed over the years is that a lot of people spend Mother's Day working on their gardens and landscaping. At least here in Boston, Mother's Day is when the garden nurseries are finally fully stocked and selling all the good plants and flowers you had been waiting all winter for. If there's good weather, you can spend that weekend gardening.

When it comes down to it, Mother's Day and Father's Day are just Spring and Summer weekends where most people don't have competing plans. You can take advantage of this by planning a special outing or weekend trip or day trip. If these two holidays are hard for you, it can help to plan something really fun to distract you from the sadness of your relationship with your parents.

Easter

Easter is another holiday where people tend to celebrate it by having dinner with their family and extended family. As we've already discussed, holiday dinners can often be a time of stress or heartache for those from toxic families. If you're looking to do something different and more fun, I have some ideas for you!

If Easter is a religious holiday for you, then it might be fun and uplifting to go to a sunrise service at your church. Many churches have various activities going on all day on Easter. Going to church and then having a special dinner with your significant other or church friends may be a far better way to celebrate the holiday.

If you are not religious, there are still great options for you. Growing up, Easter was a fun time for me to do craft projects. I loved dying the eggs and making paper decorations. As an adult, dying eggs doesn't appeal to me anymore, but I still love doing crafts. If you also love doing crafts or being artistic, why not devote the day to doing a craft that you love?

Easter Sunday can be a great day to do some activity that you love. If you have friends that are in the same boat as you with their family, you could also invite them to do something fun together. Local businesses seem to have caught on to the fact that not everyone spends the holidays with their family and there seems to be more and more special events being held on the holidays. Check out your town's event calendar. You might be surprised at all of the fun things going on during the holidays.

Your Birthday

For a lot of people from dysfunctional families, memories of childhood birthdays are very painful. There was often a family member that didn't like you being in the spotlight and had to ruin it for you, or it was simply disappointing because of the behavior of your family on what was supposed to be a special day. Perhaps you are like my client Danielle and you stopped celebrating your birthday all together.

When Danielle was 9 years old, no one showed up to her birthday party. Previous to this experience, she was friends with just about all of the neighborhood kids and they would all come to her birthday parties and she would go to theirs. Then that year, no one came.

Danielle had handed out invitations and everything seemed normal, then that day no one showed up. She spent the day looking out the window, waiting for the doorbell to ring. Her parents didn't handle the situation well. They were not sympathetic to Danielle's plight and simply let her look out the window all day while they went about the rest of their business.

At the time, Danielle felt deeply embarrassed and ashamed about the situation. She did approach her best friend and asked her why she didn't show up to the party. Her friend just said "Oh, my mom and dad took me out that day. I was gone all day." Her friend didn't seem to care or be apologetic about it, so Danielle decided it was best to simply never talk about it again. She felt rejected and very confused about what happened.

The next year she told her parents that she didn't want to have a party and they were perfectly fine with that. They gave her a gift and that was that. Most parents would have perhaps been concerned about the situation or at least talked to their child about it, but not Danielle's parents. She never had a birthday party again.

As an adult, Danielle didn't tell her friends what day her birthday was. Sure, she went to their birthday get-togethers, but never had one of her own. Her friends never asked if she had a birthday coming up, so she figured that they didn't care just like everyone else. She would work on her birthday and treat it as just an ordinary day, but part of her did feel bad that she didn't have friends that would plan to do something fun with her on her birthday.

Through therapy, Danielle realized what went wrong on her birthday so many years ago. It was during that time around when she was 9 that her parent's marriage was self-destructing. The incidents of domestic violence were becoming so frequent and so intense that her parents could no longer hide it from the neighborhood. Her friend's parents stopped allowing them to go over Danielle's house around that time. The birthday party was held at Danielle's house.

At the time, Danielle couldn't understand why her friends stopped coming over, but as an adult it made perfect sense. She wouldn't let her own children go over a house like that so she couldn't blame her friend's parents anymore. It was such a relief to know that that was the reason why her friends starting distancing themselves from her. Danielle had blamed herself for so long, but it wasn't her fault, it was her parent's.

Ultimately, Danielle decided that she was going to celebrate her birthday again, but it was going to be on her terms. The idea of having a party still didn't appeal to her but she decided she would take the day off of work and do something really special this year and each year going forward. You can do something similar to Danielle. Your birthday is about you. Do something that would be special for you.

Their Birthday

For some toxic family members, their birthday is an excuse to hold the family hostage and act like Divas. If you still have contact with these family members, you may be wondering how to navigate this situation.

First, have you been invited to any specific family gathering for your relative's birthday or does "anything go"? If there are no plans or invitations, then that's a good thing. It pretty much means that you can handle the birthday in whichever manner makes the most sense to you. As discussed previously, often toxic family members are better when seen on an individual basis. It may mean that you can take them out for a birthday dinner one on one and avoid the drama of a big get together.

Secondly, if there is a big get-together, how do other family members handle it? Are there people who show up late and leave early? Are there people who don't go at all? If so, why do you think that these people get a free pass? Are there things you can do to also be excused from the event if you don't want to go? If attendance is mandatory in your family, try to find a way to avoid spending a significant amount of time with the trouble makers in the family. A good strategy is to bring a game or activity and immerse yourself in it with the non-trouble-making people at the event, then quietly duck out when things are winding down.

Depending on your family's traditions and family-culture, it may be sufficient to simply mail a card or a gift. For a lot of families, mailing a card or gift is seen as "doing your duty" to the family and is considered enough. Hopefully it will be seen as enough in your family, but only you can really be the judge of this.

Creating new traditions

One of the hardest parts about limiting contact or ending contact with a dysfunctional family is the loss of traditions. Although some people may argue that family traditions are pointless and no one really cares about them, a lot of people do care. As human beings, we generally need two things in order to feel happy: The first thing we need is spontaneity and novelty. The second thing we need is routine and traditions.

We need spontaneity and novelty because it adds a sense of fun and adventure to our lives. Routine and tradition helps to add a sense of safety and security in our life. If we have too much routine, we can become bored and listless. We will feel like something's missing and we may even feel depressed. If we have too much spontaneity, we will feel restless and anxious. We will feel like we're flying by the seat of our pants and we won't like it. So, we need a balance of both.

Upon initially pulling away from your dysfunctional family, you can feel a void left from the loss of routine and tradition. This can be especially difficult if you are reducing contact in a very enmeshed family. Some families are so enmeshed that when you reduce contact or end contact entirely, it can feel like you are left with *nothing*. It can be very helpful to create new traditions and new routines with your immediate family, significant other, and friends.

We already discussed the ways that you can create new holiday traditions, but I believe traditions go much deeper and it's important to recognize this and to try to fill this void as well. In addition to holiday traditions, people and families often have traditions of daily living. For instance, my mother had an antique food grinder that was given to her from her grandmother. It was probably a hundred years old. As a child it fascinated me to watch her pour the cranberries into it and turn the handle and see cranberry relish come out of it. Well, sometime during a move, the grinder was lost.

Now, some may say "It was just a food grinder, who cares?" but for me this was a sentimental piece of my childhood and seeing it attached to a kitchen counter was an important tradition for me. So, I went to an antiques market and bought my own! I found one that looks just like the original and using it gives me a sense of joy. I was able to bring back a tradition I loved from my childhood.

I've also created my own traditions of having special dishes and dishware. I've collected vintage dishware and serving pieces from thrift stores and antique markets. I don't know what it is exactly, but for me this has created a sense of tradition and family within my home. I also think my husband would agree that it just wouldn't be a casserole if it wasn't served in a vintage Pyrex casserole dish!

After my husband and I got married, we have come up with many other traditions that have helped up to create our own sense of family between the two of us. I actually found the process of creating new traditions to be a lot of fun. What are some things that you could do to create your own traditions and routines? If vintage and antique housewares don't do anything for you, then what about having special Sunday dinners or going for walks in the evening?

We have to remember that the reason why things became family traditions in the first place is because somebody initially liked them and decided to do them on a regular basis. That food grinder became a tradition in my family probably because my mother enjoyed watching her grandmother use it just like I enjoyed watching my mother use it. The same is true for the traditions in your family of origin. You can choose to keep doing the things that you enjoyed growing up in your family (Like I did, by purchasing my own grinder) and you can disregard the things that you don't like.

Remember, it's not sacrilegious to disregard a family tradition. These traditions only started because one of your relatives at some point liked it. If you don't personally like a certain tradition, then there's really no point in continuing to do it. This is an opportunity for you to create your own traditions just like your parents and grandparents did when they became adults. There is nothing wrong with you creating your own traditions.

The first time you change a change tradition (such as no longer participating in the family gift-exchange at Christmas) you will probably feel some anxiety about it. From your family's perspective, you are doing some radical and they will try to discourage you. But after you successfully stop doing a tradition that causes you stress you will feel really good about it. Eliminating stressful family traditions and replacing them with things you enjoy has a very freeing effect on your life.

So, you are about to embark on an exciting time in your life. Right now, anything is possible. You can start to create a life with traditions and spontaneity that add fun and give your life meaning. Remember, this is why you wanted to be an adult when you were a kid, so you could craft your own life. Now's the time to start doing it. What new tradition will you try out this week?

10

Stop Auditioning!

The overall impression that Vanessa got growing up was that who she was as a person was unacceptable. She was rejected by her family, rejected by other kids at school, and she was a loner in general. Growing up she never had more than one friend at a time. She would seek out other loners and befriend them. It was a no-risk strategy that worked well for her, but eventually these friends would want more and when they found other friends they would leave her behind.

Freshman year of college, Vanessa got sick of always being alone. She was in college now and really wanted to have that "college experience". She didn't want to look back at her years of college and say "Yep, I did nothing but study and wander around campus alone." As much as she wanted to have a social life, she also didn't want to be rejected. She decided to study other people very carefully. She made careful note of who was popular and who wasn't. She also made note of why some people were popular and others weren't. Based on these observations, she made a list of rules for herself in how she interacted with others.

Once Vanessa had reinvented herself according to the "rules" she had made, she found that it didn't take long before she had made a group of friends. For the first time in her life, she was being invited to parties! She had eight friends now! She was having the time of her life and loving it, and then something happened. Vanessa described it as a "social bomb". Everything just suddenly blew up.

One of the female "friends" in the group decided she didn't like Vanessa. Vanessa started hearing rumors from some other people in the group that Julie was talking about her. No one would tell her what Julie was saying exactly, just that it wasn't good. Vanessa noticed that she was no longer being invited to these get-togethers and she was being snubbed by people in the group.

She finally discovered what Julie was saying about her because she was lucky enough to catch her in the act. As she approached the cafeteria, she saw Julie talking with two other people in the group. She ducked behind a column and listened. Julie was saying outrageous things about her. They were outright lies about her sleeping with Julie's boyfriend and being a drug addict amongst other things. Vanessa was shocked; how could someone lie like that? It was just like how Vanessa's older sister would lie about her to her mother.

Vanessa couldn't let this stand. She had worked too hard to get a group of friends. She waited until she got Julie alone and confronted her. Julie just sat there in silence. Julie knew she was caught and she knew there was nothing she could say to deny it. Vanessa thought that would be the end of it, but it actually just encouraged Julie to take things even further. Within a week after confronting Julie, Vanessa had no friends. Once again, she had been completely rejected. Everyone believed Julie because she had been in the group longer. Vanessa was the "new comer". It was probably also hard for people to believe that someone could blatantly lie in the way Julie did.

For at least a year after the social bomb, Vanessa stopped trying to make any friends. Now, more than ever before in her life, she was truly a loner. She went to school, studied, and went to bed. She was truly alone and she became very depressed. Vanessa was so depressed that she was at times suicidal. Between her frequent thoughts of suicide and over-sleeping, she doesn't know how she made it through that first year of college.

She decided, once again, that she needed to make friends. This time she realized that it didn't matter what you did, there would always be someone out there who hated you, as Julie did. It wasn't enough to be "most things to most people". She decided she needed a different strategy. Julie decided that she would try customizing herself for each individual. She had heard the term "social chameleon" before and sought out becoming one. She practiced and experimented until she had perfected the art. By the time she finished college and got her Real estate license, Vanessa was able to change her personality automatically without even having to think about it.

This skill made her a great Real estate agent. She was considered to be one of the best agents at the agency she worked for. She found herself with many great acquaintances and was liked by her co-workers. She was married to a wonderful man who didn't seem to notice, or at least never said anything about Vanessa's propensity to change her personality depending on whom she was in contact with.

Although everyone seemed to like Vanessa, she had no friends. The problem with being a social chameleon is you can't really hang out in a group because you don't know how to act. Vanessa was terrified of other people finding out her "secret" so she never let anyone too close. Her husband never judged her for this as he was also an introvert and seemed happy just spending most of his time with Vanessa. In fact, the two had eloped to avoid the social awkwardness of a wedding.

One day Vanessa was talking with a co-worker in the hallways at the Real estate office. Another co-worker walked by and Vanessa instantly changed her personality. The other co-worker then had an uncomfortable look on her face and said quietly "You're acting strange right now". Vanessa didn't know what to say and the other co-worker just walked away. The co-worker stopped talking with her after that. Vanessa had been found out.

She was at a point in her life where she really didn't care about being popular anymore. However, changing her personality to better suit other people had become almost automatic and instantaneous. She wanted to stop, but she also didn't know who the real her was anymore. She wanted to say that the "real her" was the personality she had with her husband but she wasn't sure. Vanessa finally decided that it was time to see a therapist.

The therapist helped Vanessa to understand that the person she was before she went to college and started experimenting with ways to make friends, the person who was always rejected and the person she didn't like, wasn't the real her either. That part of her was heavily influenced by her dysfunctional family. Her family had shaped her into a timid and awkward person who was always afraid of saying the wrong thing. That wasn't the real her.

Through therapy, Vanessa was able to peel back the layers of dysfunction given to her by her family. She realized that she was actually an extrovert, but had become an introvert in order to save herself the pain of being rejected. She discovered that the real her had a love of spontaneity and a quirky sense of humor. Is that personality everyone's cup of tea? No. But Vanessa didn't care. Some people will like her for the "real her" and some people won't, and that's okay. She learned that it's unreasonable to expect that everyone will like her and want to be her friend.

Vanessa and her therapist decided that it was best that she started working at another agency. She was able to be her true self. Slowly Vanessa started making real friends. It took time, but it did happen. For the first time in her life, she had a social life. Even her introverted husband started being more social.

Anything really good in life takes time and there are no short cuts, but with time Vanessa discovered her true self and grew a circle of genuine friendships. She had an active social life and was truly happy. Her lifelong depression and social anxiety lifted. She could finally be her authentic self and she liked herself as a person.

Maybe you can't relate completely to Vanessa's story, but you can probably relate to parts of it, especially the part about feeling that socially you are unacceptable. This is a problem that I encounter many times with my clients that come from dysfunctional families. Socially, they feel completely inept. They have also had many painful rejection and bullying experiences.

What happens is that they are rejected by their dysfunctional families, and then they are rejected by other kids at school, perhaps later on they are bullied by a co-worker in the office. For people with this experience, the thought is "Perhaps my family is right. Maybe who I am as a person really is unacceptable". It's so painful to be rejected in this manner that people naturally try to look for a reason so they can change it. They examine their behavior and interactions with other people and it seems normal, but if it's normal, why do they keep being rejected?

They can't quite figure out what they are doing wrong, but they are the common denominator in all these painful experiences so they decide that there must be something wrong with them that is causing all of these problems. They decide that they are just "defective" or "cursed" to always be someone that other people don't like. Once people decide this about themselves, there are in general two paths they take: One way is that they become virtual hermits; they avoid other people as much as possible. The second strategy is they do what Vanessa did, they try to change who they are to suit other people: they audition.

Auditioning

Traditionally speaking, people "audition" by putting themselves up on a stage and try acting in a certain way in order for other people to accept them for a certain role. Although this usually refers to aspiring actors, if you come from a dysfunctional family, you may have been auditioning your whole life. We've already discussed how in dysfunctional families people get forced into certain roles. Back then, you didn't have to audition for that role, it was just put upon you and if you tried to act contrary to the parameters of that role, there were negative consequences.

It goes without saying that people from dysfunctional families can become comfortable with the idea of being in a role. Let's say that there's someone named Alissa who goes to school with you, works with you, or lives in your same building. Alissa seems to be the life of the party and just a cool person in general. You decide that you would really like to be her friend. How do you go about this?

The way people from functional families go about this is they will try to have a chat with Alissa to get to know her better. They will ask her what kind of things she likes to do for fun to see if they have common interests. While doing this, they will also be paying attention to how easy it is to talk with Alissa. *Does the conversation flow easily? Do our personalities mesh well?* If it turns out that they have common interests and have compatible personalities, they will then invite Alissa to do one of those common interests with them in the near future. If not, they will decide that they just aren't compatible as friends, say "Well, it's been nice talking to you" and part amicably.

People from dysfunctional families often take a different approach. Instead, they will audition for the role of "Alissa's friend". They will try to ascertain what Alissa is looking for in a friend and then try to become that person, even if it is not true to who they are as an individual. Just like an actor trying to win the role of "Alissa's friend" in a TV show, you try to win the real life role by morphing yourself into what you think Alissa wants. You do everything you can to try to prove to her that you are worthy of this role, *because hey, you wouldn't be worthy otherwise.*

The difference between these two strategies is that people from functional families are looking for a mutually beneficial relationship with Alissa. They're trying to see if *both* of them would enjoy each other's company. And if not, *oh well*. They view their enjoyment of the relationship as being just as important as Alissa's. The stakes are very low for the person from a functional family. If they become friends with Alissa, then that's great! If not, then there are plenty of other people they could try to be friends with.

For people from dysfunctional families, the stakes are very high because they feel as though their self-esteem depends on Alissa's approval. To them, if Alissa accepted their friendship, it would mean that they are finally worthy or acceptable, it doesn't matter how phony they had to be to win that role. It doesn't matter that the whole relationship is based on Alissa's enjoyment, because it's enough for them to be finally accepted for once in their life.

Not everyone takes "auditioning" to the extreme that Vanessa did. Some people only do it for their families or certain other people that they feel they would get a self-esteem boost from. Becoming a true "social chameleon" like Vanessa typically requires a person to be especially depleted to go to such extremes. In Vanessa's case this makes sense when you consider that she had decided that she as a person was completely unworthy. She had also been at the point of being suicidal, so for her the stakes were very high: literally life or death.

Although auditioning seems like a good idea at first, it has several flaws. For one, you can't let people be too close or they will discover the truth. You also usually can't spend time with more than one friend at a time. And finally, although it seems great to be accepted at first, the relationship is ultimately unsatisfying because it isn't real. Like a television show or movie, no matter how good the acting is, it is ultimately fake. You will still have a void in your life from where real friendship could have been.

Another problem with auditioning is that it's also not an effective means of building self-esteem. Sure, you may feel an initial self-esteem boost in the moment, but it quickly fades. Like an addict, you're constantly looking for your next fix. You are always in need of achievements, reassurance, and affirmation that you are a worthy person. If this is what you do to try to build your self-esteem, then the building will never end.

The difference between people with low self-esteem and people with high self-esteem is that the people with low self-esteem think that self-esteem is something you win from other people. They think it's something other people can give you. It's not, but your family raised you to believe that because having that kind of influence over you made you easier to control. For people with high self-esteem, other people don't matter. If other people's opinions of them mattered, they wouldn't have high self-esteem.

They know that self-esteem is something that can only come from within.

My clients hate it when I tell them that self-esteem can only come from within. When I hear them groan, I know what they're thinking. They're thinking "Great! That means there's nothing I can do to improve my self-esteem. Apparently it's just something you're born with and I'm somebody who wasn't born with it." Here's the thing, you were born with self-esteem. Have you ever spent time with a baby? Babies think that they are the most important thing in the world. They know that they have inherent self-esteem and self-worth just for being them.

Your next question may be "If every person is born with inherent self-esteem and self-worth, then why do some people have such low self-esteem?" The answer is that somewhere along the way you were taught that you didn't have self-worth. Other people took it from you and you've been waiting for them to give it back. Those people were probably initially your family members.

Your family took it away and you started to try to get it back by being "extra good" as a child or in some other way auditioning for the role of "valued child" or "loved child". Children from these environments, despite how hard they try to fit in, behave in ways that give themselves away. Other children can tell that there's something "off" about them and respond accordingly. This social rejection just reinforces the low self-esteem further.

People can tell when other people don't respect themselves and for some reason, people seem to feel a natural aversion to such people. It's an odd thing, if you think about it. You would think that people would respond with compassion and a desire to help such a person, and although some people do, most people respond with the opposite response. It's something that's very confusing for the person on the receiving end.

People mistreat you, not because they believe that you are unworthy, but because *you* do. You believe that you deserve to be rejected, so other people do too. People treat you according to the way that you decide that you deserve to be treated. Once you find that inner self-esteem, you'd be amazed at the way that others start treating you. It's definitely different, and a whole lot better.

Aside from the fact that auditioning doesn't really work, as we discussed earlier, another problem with it is that it cheapens you. Whenever we try to be something else, we'll only ever be a cheap copy. Instead we should strive to be the best "us" we can be. If you really embraced who you are as an individual, you could become the greatest "you" anyone has ever seen. A cheap copy will never be described as "great", but *you* could be great. It comes with embracing yourself. So stop auditioning!

Modern day hermits

I wrote in the beginning of the chapter that people generally take two paths, one is to audition and the other is to become a virtual hermit. There is of course the possibility that people do a little of both or have had periods in their life where they have alternated between the two. Due to this, I would like to address this path as well.

Before the modern age, a hermit was someone who broke off from society. They would go to a cave or live off in the forest away from everyone. They would use their time to pray, study, or otherwise gain wisdom. There have been a few notable modern day hermits: Christopher McCandless inspired the book and movie "Into the Wild". He traveled the country as a homeless person before eventually making his way into the Alaskan Wilderness in order to escape other people entirely. Author J. D. Salinger did not disappear into the wild, but he did disappear into a small town in New Hampshire where he is said to have been extremely private.

When people look at these types of people, they often assume that they were merely extreme introverts. I think that this is true in some cases, but not all. Let me explain: Most people measure whether a person in an introvert or extravert by how much time they spend in the company of other people, by how "outgoing" their personality is. However, this is not a true measure of extraversion or introversion.

The actual difference between introversion and extraversion is not how you act, but how you feel. Introverts feel drained by other people, whereas extraverts feel energized. Introverts become energized by spending time in solitude. Extraverts feel drained by spending too much time alone. Another thing is you don't want to confuse feeling "drained" for social anxiety, because that's a different thing entirely. Fears of embarrassing yourself or being judged are not the same as feeling drained by being in the company of others.

Many of my clients whom were raised in toxic families were surprised to find that they were actually extraverts. Once they resolved their family issues and alleviated their social anxiety and fears of being rejected, they realized that they actually very much enjoyed being social. You may still be an introvert, but perhaps not as much of an introvert as you once thought you were.

And by the way, there's nothing wrong with being an introvert, but let's not confuse introversion for something it's not. Many modern day hermits, such as Salinger and McCandless, are not introverts but rather people who had such painful experiences that they decided that "hell is other people". Perhaps they would have liked to be close to others but had simply had too many painful experiences. Which do you think it is for you? Are you an introvert or are you really just scared of being rejected?

Let me share my own experience. I was never someone that went to dances. When I went to my prom, I didn't dance. I didn't dance because I believed that I couldn't do it. You see, no one had ever taught me and the few times I had tried to get up and dance, it didn't go well and I felt that I had embarrassed myself. I told myself "I just don't have rhythm. I can't dance."

There's probably a good decade or more in everyone's life where having a good social life depends on one's ability to get up and dance. At the prom, at weddings, at the office Christmas Party, I sat at the table and watched while everyone else danced. To make myself feel better I told myself "Its okay, not everyone likes dancing.   Different people like different activities and there's nothing wrong with that". The problem was I *did* like dancing. I wanted to get up there and dance, but I was too afraid of embarrassing myself in a crowd of people.

I finally decided to do something about it. I took lessons and I started practicing for about a half hour every night. A week after I started practicing, I went to a social dancing event and got up on the dance floor and danced for three songs. I was not even close to being the best dancer there, but I was dancing! I kept practicing and two weeks later I went to another event and danced for an hour and a half. I've kept with it and now I go to social dancing events all the time and it looks like I took lessons for years.

I bring this up because I learned something important from that experience that I think you can possibly relate to. When we grow up in dysfunctional families, it can feel like we're way behind other people in terms of social skills and life skills. None of my parents ever danced. We never held a family get-together where a relative would turn on some music and people would start dancing, providing a safe and supportive place for a young child to learn how to dance. Instead, my first experience was in Junior High when they were holding an afterschool dance.

Of course it didn't go well! I realize now that trying to learn how to dance at the school dance is like trying to learn how to play an instrument at the recital. At the time though all I saw was everyone else dancing and I felt like a clumsy idiot. Why could everyone else dance so easily and I could do nothing? It was such a humiliating experience that it kept me from dancing again until I was in my 30s.

Maybe you can't relate to my struggles with dancing socially, but perhaps you can relate to other social situations that are very difficult for you. It can seem like being social is so easy for other people, yet you find yourself constantly in fear of embarrassing yourself or screwing up. It can seem like the safest thing to do is to just avoid so situations as much as possible.

Here's the thing though; you are not inept. I thought that I was inept when it came to dancing and boy was I wrong. All I needed was some lessons and some practice. You just need the same thing. Most people get taught these social lessons by their parents at a very young age and that's why it comes easy for them. For whatever reason, your parents didn't teach you those things, but it's not too late to learn them now. As a therapist, I teach adults social skills all the time. It's something that can be picked up rather easily once you have someone willing to teach you.

There's another thing that I think is important for people to recognize and that is that you are not in High School anymore. When the thought of dancing came up in mind, it was like I was transported back to that Junior High dance. I assumed that I would get the same strange looks, snickers, and mean comments I got back then. The thing is though, that was back in Junior High. Adults don't act like that.

You'll remember that in Vanessa's story she had a pretty bad experience in college. Although we like to think of college students as being adults, for the first two years of college, most of them are still teenagers. Although many find college to be infinitely better than High School, you can still expect to encounter many of the same teenage behaviors you did in High School, so please don't let any negative college experiences discourage you either.

At my first social dance, although I had only had a week to practice, I found everyone to be really nice and really encouraging. What a different experience from Junior High School! I've also had the opportunity to view other adults who are beginner dancers too and have struggled to get on the dance floor for the first time. What I've realized is that every great dancer had that first dance experience where they weren't good and it took a longtime before they got good. The same is true with other social activities.

The nice thing about learning these things as an adult is that no one's going to make fun of you. Actually, if you go somewhere and another adult makes fun of you because you are still learning, then you need to go to another venue because that one is horrible. No adult should be making fun of another adult because that is extremely childish and immature. Any adult who makes fun of you has something wrong with them, not you.

If you've found yourself jealous of the social lives of other people, then I want you to turn that jealousy into action: Start going to these social events that you've always wanted to go to and come up with a plan ahead of time to deal with any anxiety associated with the event. Find someone you trust and help them coach you through any part of it that you might find difficult at first. You'll find that having a plan will greatly alleviate your anxiety. If you can't find someone to be your social coach, consider seeing a therapist. Once you start putting yourself out there, you'll be glad you did and you'll find that being social gets easier the more you do it.

Conclusion

Although you were raised to believe you were unacceptable, that isn't true. You have your own unique personality. You have your own strengths and weaknesses and those are the special gifts that you bring to social situations.

Like Vanessa, you may feel like you've figured out how to shape your personality to be more pleasing to other people, and that's probably a good skill to have if you're trying to sell real estate, but it's a disaster if you want to make real friends. Or perhaps you stopped auditioning for other people long ago and have decided that it's better to just be alone in order to avoid painful social encounters. Either way, I want you to remember that actually the best way to avoid rejection and to have great friendships is to just *be you*.

I'm sure right now that the advice to "just be yourself" sounds like a bunch of bullshit and I'm sure you've heard it before, but there's a reason why everyone says it. Because it works! When we are true to ourselves and focus on being the best "us" we can be, rather than try to be a cheap imitation of what's popular, we attract the right kinds of people into our lives. We attract people who like us for us and have complimentary personalities and interests.   In other words, we create mutually beneficial and genuine friendships.

There is actually a principle used in marketing called "sales prevention". If you're selling a product, you of course want to sell as much of it as possible, but you also don't want to sell it to the wrong people. The "wrong people" are people who won't fully appreciate your product. They're just not right for the product. So, marketers will slip things into their advertising to purposefully turn some people away. There's actually a popular phrase in marketing that "If you're selling to everybody, you're selling to nobody".

As Vanessa discovered, if you're trying to be friends with everybody, you're friends with nobody. It doesn't matter how nice and awesome of a person you are, there's still going to be people who don't want to be your friend, and perhaps even people who hate you. And you know what, who cares? When someone rejects me, I feel like I dodged a bullet just as much as they do. I don't want to waste my time and effort working on a friendship with someone who ultimately isn't worth my time either.

If you don't believe me that it's impossible to make everyone like you, I want you to think of your favorite book. Now I want you to go look up the reviews for it. I bet you there's at least one person who absolutely hated the book. There are books that are considered to be masterpieces that people absolutely hate, but just because some people hated the book does that mean that the book shouldn't have been written?   No, because there are also plenty of people who absolutely loved it.

I discovered this when I first started writing my own books. My first book was called "Couples Counseling: A step by step guide for therapists". I poured my heart into that book, but I was so scared of getting negative reviews that I held off on publishing it for a long time. I felt like I had put so much effort into the book that if it was not well received that it would be crushing. Well, I eventually published it and can you guess what happened?

After the book was published, the reviews started trickling in and it seemed that it was very well received. I was getting five star reviews and that just warmed my heart. Then I got a one star review. The review was so negative I was actually wondering if I went to High School with the person who wrote it. It was clear from the review that she *hated* the book and she *hated me* for having written it. I went back through the book to try to see what I could have written to have offended this person so much. You know what? I never did find what upset that person so much.

I've decided since then that it doesn't matter. I put my best effort into all the books I write and I'm proud of that. I don't try to write in a manner that's "popular", because that's not me. I write in a manner that's true to myself and genuine. I try to write in such a way that reading one of my books is just like having a real conversation with me. In other words, I try to be the best "me" I can be and make no apologies if some people don't like it. There are always going to be people who don't like it and that just means my writing style is not their cup of tea, and that's okay!

Not everyone's going to like the real you, and that's okay too. But the people who do like you, will like you for you and will be people that you truly enjoy sharing your life with. In my opinion that's so much better than trying to appeal to everybody. So stop auditioning and start enjoying your life and other people.

11

You are enough

Will's father left when he was a baby. His whole life it was just him, his older sister, and his mother. They never had any extended family, and although he never questioned it as a child, he realized as he got older that it was probably because his extended family had disowned his mother. His mother was a volatile person and a drug addict. It was not pleasant to be around her and for the most part, everyone avoided her.

He could often find his mother laying across the couch with a talk show on TV. Sometimes there were other people with her and they would all be sitting in the living room doing drugs together. Will would try to sneak past them so he could quickly get inside his bedroom and get away from all of them. One time, one of the guys his mother was with stopped him.

He pulled Will aside and asked him if he wanted to be in a movie. Everyone was smiling and being nice to him for once, even his mother. Will had a bad feeling about this, but felt like he couldn't say no. He tentatively agreed. The man set up a video camera and Will ended up being raped and molested by him and another man. Afterwards the man gave his mother some $20's and a bag of cocaine. She seemed pleased, and then yelled at Will to go to his room. Will was only 12 years old.

Will's mother had traded his childhood for drugs. It was a difficult reality for him to accept. He became filled with rage. He was no longer going to be the passive and complicit son. When he was 14 he assaulted his mother and got sent to Juvenile detention. When he got out, he started selling drugs to other kids at school and around the neighborhood. He put zero effort into his school work and rather than keep repeating Freshman year, he dropped out of school at 16.

At age 17, his mother moved to Florida to be with a boyfriend. He just came home one day and saw that she was gone. Will's sister and he tried to keep the apartment for as long as they could, but eventually they went their separate ways. He needed to make enough money to support himself but he had no skills and no education and even if he worked over-time, he could never make enough money at a retail job to support himself. The solution came to Will almost serendipitously.

Will was approached by some other drug dealers he knew. They encouraged him to join them. They told him that they could all work together and look out for each other. It meant more money and less risk than being on his own. Will agreed. What he didn't realize at the time was that he was agreeing to join a gang.

At first, Will found that life in a gang suited him. For the first time in his life he felt accepted. He received approval and encouragement. It was like the family he never had, and Will was fiercely loyal. He became well known for his loyalty. Nothing they asked of him was out of the question. He went to prison several times but didn't care. To him, it well worth it. At least at first it was.

At 25 years old, it wasn't fun anymore. He was one of the oldest people in the gang and he knew it was rare for a gang member to live past 30 and if they did, it was because they were serving a life sentence in prison. He decided he didn't want that to be him. He was lucky, the gang allowed him to leave. Once again, Will found himself on his own. He tried contacting his mother and sister but they wanted nothing to do with him. Finally, he went to the welfare office.

Will felt disgusted with himself. Here he was at 25 years old living off of welfare in government housing. He couldn't even get a retail job because of his criminal background. Since leaving the gang he had also developed crippling social anxiety. He felt completely worthless. One of the social workers at the welfare office encouraged him to see a therapist. She gave him a referral to the local community mental health center and despite his better judgment, he actually went.

Seeing the therapist was actually the best decision that Will ever made. The therapist helped Will with his anxiety, low self-esteem, and trauma from having been raped as a child. Even still, Will felt worthless as a human being. He felt as though he was only in his 20s but had already ruined his life. He had no education and no ability to get a job. He had no job skills. He reminisced that the only thing he was ever good at was dealing drugs. He was the best dealer in the city and he knew he could make quick money if he took it up again. To him it seemed that his only choices were start dealing and probably die young or be a worthless drain on society.

His therapist pointed out that Will actually did have a skill: dealing. He was really good at selling; why not go into business for himself? In that moment, a light bulb went off in Will's head. He could actually do this. Will only had $20 to start his business with, but he was determined. It was at least worth a try.

You wouldn't think an ex-gang member would have an eye for antiques and vintage home goods, but Will actually did. Will really liked antiques because they reminded him of a hominess and wholesomeness that he never got from his own family. He would pick things up at a yard sale for $1 and then sell it online for $30. Some things he even got for free off the curb. He would use the computers at the library to sell his merchandise.

The therapist was right, he was good at selling. At first he just used his profits to buy more antiques until he had acquired a sizeable inventory. Once that happened, he realized he was now making a steady income. Will moved into his first real apartment. He soon found that if he wanted to make more money, he would need to hire some workers. Will hired other reformed gang members and bought storage space.

His business was both a second chance for him, a second chance for the people who worked for him, and a second chance for the once discarded items he was selling. The local news did a story on Will and his business and after that, business soared. Although *at age 25 he was doing comparatively worse than his peers, at age 30 he was doing comparatively better. Even Will was shocked by what he had accomplished for himself.*

For the first time in his life, he felt that he was enough. He at first tried to contribute his new found self-esteem to what he had accomplished, but he realized that wasn't it. He had accomplished what he had accomplished because he had already had self-esteem. Self-esteem was a cause of his success, not a result of it. He was only able to do what he did because he believed he was worthy of it. Will realized that self-esteem was something he had always had, but at certain times in his life it was buried.

Like all children, he was born with self-esteem. Every time his mother ignored him or put him down, it was buried a little more. When he was raped, it was buried further. When he found himself destitute at 25, it was buried so deep he didn't think he would ever find it again, but it was always there. He was always enough; he just sadly didn't recognize it until he was 30 years old.

In the last chapter, I introduced the concept that self-esteem can neither be given to you nor earned, it's something found within. It's something we are all born with and all have. Just by being you, you are worthy. Despite what anyone else says, you are enough.

The question I often get asked is "So if we're all born with high self-esteem, then why do some people end up with such low self-esteem?" Low self-esteem comes from a belief that other people's opinions about you matter; that other people's approval or disapproval determines your worth. People with low self-esteem believe that if other people approve of them, then it means that they are "worthy" and they feel a little temporary boost to their self- esteem. When other people express criticism or disapproval, they feel a hit to their self-esteem and decide that they are "unworthy".

Everyone, even people with very high self-esteem, has experienced many experiences of rejection during their life. The difference is that they look at it differently. Someone with high self-esteem may feel bad about the rejection for a while but then decide that it doesn't really matter because there are other people out there who won't reject them. They feel confident in their self-worth and know that they have a lot to offer other people. People with low self-esteem see the rejection as being part of a continuous pattern of rejection in their life; mounting evidence that they are indeed unworthy.

You see, people with low self-esteem have a little voice in their head that tells them that they aren't good enough. Whenever they think about doing something nice for themselves the voice says "Nice things like that are for other people, not people like you". Whenever they consider doing something social the voice says "Everyone's going to wonder why you're there. They're going to be able to tell that you don't belong". When you think about starting your own business or trying to advance your career it says "You don't have what it takes to succeed. You're going to fail and then everyone will know what a failure you are".

The greatest day of your life will be the day when you tell that little voice to "shut the fuck up" and it finally shuts the fuck up forever. Will always had the ability to succeed in business, but the little voice convinced him that he couldn't. It convinced him that being in a gang and taking the fall for other people was all he was good for. It wasn't until he told that voice to shut up that he was able to do what he always could.

Where the voice came from

The "voice" sounds like it's coming from us, but it didn't originate with us. The voice developed somewhere in our child-hood, often early on in life.

I said earlier that children are born with high self-esteem. There is no little voice telling them that they are not good enough. That comes later, but how and from where? If you were raised in a dysfunctional family, then it's very likely that that voice originated with your parents.

When we're kids, we don't know anything about the world. We come equipped with a few things that help with basic survival, but we know nothing about how the world works nor do we know anything of social nuances. We need to be taught those things from our parents and other kids. The primary educators in our life are first our parents, then our siblings, then our peers, then adults other than our parents. So we absolutely depend on our parents and families to teach us who we are and how we fit into the world. It goes without saying that it is thus extremely damaging for a child if that family is toxic.

Little kids are sponges. They pick up on absolutely everything. I can remember moments in my childhood where it is clear that my father intended for those moments to be "teaching moments". He was using an opportunity to try to shape my future adult self. There were also plenty of moments where he did not intend them to be teaching moments (and probably would have preferred that I wasn't watching) where he was just trying to get by in his day. However, all of these were "teaching moments", and probably in ways that he did not intend them to be.

Children are constantly observing and constantly learning. Through these observations we start to develop little rules that help us navigate the world in a manner that we hope will maximize our happiness and help us to avoid pain. Once these rules are set, they are extremely rigid and follow us into adulthood. They can be changed, but it takes deliberate effort.

Let's go back to Will to better illustrate this point. After Will was sexually assaulted, he instantly developed new rules about the world. He had previously had a rule that he should be complacent and subservient to his mother. After the rape, he abandoned that rule because it led to him experiencing a terrible amount of pain and trauma. He then decided that he couldn't trust or respect his mother anymore. He also decided that the only thing he was good for was fulfilling other people's needs. The only time in his childhood that adults seemed to like him or want him around was the time he was being abused. So Will then acted upon this belief by being the perpetual "fall guy" for his gang. It wasn't about his needs; it was about everyone else's.

Some rules we develop in childhood are good and they help us to become functioning adults. Some rules, especially those developed in a dysfunctional family, hinder us from becoming a functioning adult. It's important to remember that even if these rules seem to be holding you back as an adult, they were probably useful in childhood. As a child, it was good that Will stopped trusting his mother. If he had continued to be complacent and trusting of her he may not have survived his childhood.

What rules about the world did you develop as a child? Although they may have helped you to survive in a toxic family, are they now hurting and hindering you as an adult? How can you change those rules to more adequately reflect the world that you are living in now?

Those rules we developed in childhood definitely become part of the voice. The other parts come from our parents and possibly our peers. When you were a child, someone told you over and over again that you weren't good enough. Although at the time it sounded like someone else's voice was saying it, after a while you internalized this message and it started to sound like your own voice. It became the little voice in your head.

Part of getting rid of that voice is recognizing where it came from. You'll remember in the last chapter I wrote how I always struggled with not knowing how to dance. The main reason why I didn't dance was, you guessed it, the little voice in my head. The voice would say "You can't dance. You're embarrassing yourself. Everyone's look at you and thinking 'who does she think she is?'" I believed this voice for a long time and it wasn't until I recognized where it came from that I was able to get rid of it.

I recognized that the things the voice said were the same things that the other kids would say to me in Junior High. Once I realized that, the whole thing seemed so ridiculous to me that I was able to silence the voice for good. I was no longer in Junior High School! I didn't have to worry about 12 year olds making fun of me anymore.

Voices that came from your parents are a little harder to get rid of since a parent's opinion has more weight than a classmate's. In situations like that, it can still help to closely examine the childhood experiences that shaped your belief system and to really process what happened. As children, we don't know anything yet and can't help but believe the things we hear our parents say. As adults, we know more and can look at things more clearly. Perhaps the conclusions you drew as a child are not the ones you would draw now.

Try to remember the experiences where the voice originates from and examine the situation very carefully. What really happened? What did you decide about it back then? What would you decide about it now? It can be extremely helpful to go through this process with a therapist.

Those that are worthy

Even after all of this, you may still have lingering issues with low self-esteem. You may not believe my theory that everyone's born with high self-esteem. You may still think that some people are more worthy than other people. This makes sense, especially if your family has a narcissist in it. The narcissist is very good at convincing people that they are better than everyone else, so you may still believe that there are people out there that are more worthy than you.

In David Burn's book "Ten Days to Self Esteem", one of the exercises involves describing the type of people whom you do believe are worthy of self-esteem. Surely in your day to day life you encounter people who you think "Wow, I bet she has high self-esteem" or "Geez, that guy has it made". These are people in your family, in your classroom, at work, or on TV that you've decided are worthy. I want you to take a moment to describe what it is about them that makes them worthy.

When I do this exercise with my clients, I've noticed that at first it's very difficult for them to give me their reasons why some people are more worthy than them. There is often a long pause before they get going, but once they start talking, I hear some very common responses. I'm going to write down those responses, as well as my rebuttal to why none of them are accurate measures for making one person more worthy than another:

- **Money:** The argument goes that money makes some people more worthy than others. This is an interesting argument because it almost implies that self-esteem is something you can buy. I imagine that if self-esteem was something you could buy, everyone would be saving up their money so they could buy it. Surely, there are already some people who do try to buy self-esteem in the form of expensive clothes and high-status items. I've actually had clients that are quite wealthy (think multi-millionaires) and they have some of the lowest self-esteem I have ever encountered. I have also had poor clients come into unexpected money (such as a million plus lottery or lawsuit winnings) although they felt happy at first; they soon went back to having low self-esteem. Money does not seem to be a cure for low self-esteem. But you may argue that you were only referring to people who earned the money through hard work; the so-called "self-made man". In situations like that, let's really think it through. If someone builds a fortune through their own hard work, and then the stock market suddenly crashes through no fault of their own, does that mean that they now deserve to lose their self-esteem? Why or why not? Another question is, do you think money is something that our society will always have? I imagine that eventually we'll reach a future where money is meaningless and everyone is essentially on equal footing financially. How will we measure self-worth then? Perhaps money is not an accurate measure of self-worth after all.

- **Attractiveness:** Many people feel that attractive people are more deserving of self-esteem than unattractive people. Once again, I have to tell you that I've had clients that were so physically attractive that they could be models, yet felt so ugly they were anxious about going out in public. So there are certainly unattractive people with high self-esteem and attractive people with low self-esteem. Another issue with attractiveness is that it's just something people are born with. Should we really judge people based on something that they can't control? It seems very unfair to me. And what about cases where someone is attractive because of plastic surgery? Does that count? I feel like attractiveness should not count in the least, and I'll tell you why: Who determines what "attractive" is? I have come across many people who would not be considered to be classically attractive (as in, you would never see them in a magazine) and yet they were so beautiful I could not keep my eyes off of them. There was just a "glow" about them. Have you ever had this experience? Believe it or not, you have probably been this person for someone else. Probably most people have. Perhaps we are all beautiful in our own unique way.
- **Confidence:** It is not surprising that "confidence" is a common response when you consider that people with low self-esteem often lack confidence themselves. What I always remind people is that unless you can read other people's minds, you have no idea how confident another person is. Probably half the people you encounter whom seem confident are not as confident as you think they are. You are judging them based on a set of behaviors that you have deemed to be indications of confidence. The thing with that is anyone can mimic behaviors. If you wanted to, you could start acting extremely confident tomorrow. So, "confidence" as you know it, really isn't that special. It's just not. I too used to have problems with not being confident, and I still am not confident in every situation, but people

would probably describe me as being a confident person. What I did was I initially just adopted the behaviors of a confident person, even though I didn't feel confident yet. What I found was that I got such positive results from acting confident that after a while I started to feel more confident too. Essentially I used the "fake it till you make it" strategy and it worked for me. You can do the same thing if you would like to be more confident.

- **Status:** Status is often tied to wealth but not always. If you're still stuck working a job you hate while your friend has recently achieved her lifelong dream of becoming a teacher, you may believe that she has a higher status than you. Some people also believe that race, marital status, gender, whether you have kids or not, religion, or sexual orientation also affect status. Status has the same problem that all of the others have in that it really doesn't matter. "Status" is just a construct invented by societies. In other words, it's just an idea that someone came up with a long time ago. Different societies have different ideas of how one achieves high status. People from different societies may think that our ideas of status are silly and vice versa. In other words, status only means something because you have convinced yourself it does.

- **Power:** Power may be related to money and status, which we've already decided are illusory. Power may also come from being in a leadership position. For instance, you may feel that a doctor has more power than his patient, or that the President has more power than the common man, but do they really? The way I see it, everyone just has different jobs and different roles to play in society. Some people might say that as a therapist I have a certain amount of power, that I have more power than my clients. I disagree with this. I need my clients just as much as they need me. Neither of us is bringing more to the table than the other. It is equal, and the same goes for other people in positions of power.

- **Does good things:** This is usually when people say "alright, alright already! But surely people who do good things deserve to have self-esteem more than people who do bad things?" Once again, I have to disagree. There is good and bad in everyone. To say that one person is "good" and another person is "bad" would require that a person be wholly good or wholly bad. I do not know of any such person. And what about Will? For a number of years he did things that people would say was "bad". Does that make him a bad person? When we just look at the actions a person takes, we are not looking at the whole picture. This may just be the therapist in me talking, but I think you need to take context into account. Going back to Will, the bad things he did were understandable given his horrific childhood. Something I've learned as a therapist is that no one does something for no reason. People usually do the things they do because given the context at the time, it seemed like the best option. There are very few people out there that are simply "evil".

The truth is no one's better than anyone else. We all have our unique mix of strengths and weaknesses. We all have a unique purpose and a unique gift to give the world. Who's to say that one person is more worthy than the other?

Comparing yourself to others

Certainly one of the biggest contributors to low self-esteem is when we compare ourselves to others. As a child, you may have been compared to a sibling or another relative that your parents thought was doing comparatively "better" than you. You may have looked at other kids at school, kids who wore nicer clothes, had more toys and friends, and wondered why you couldn't have what they had. I think that people don't realize just how early little kids start comparing themselves to others.

I have an identical twin sister and my mother had us in something called "Twin Club". Basically, it was a social group for parents of twins and they would have little social events throughout the year. One year we went to their Christmas party. One of the dads in the group dressed like Santa Clause and handed out a gift to each child that was there. I know now that those gifts were bought by each child's parent, but at the time I really believed that they were coming from Santa Clause.

I looked around at what gifts the other children got, and they looked like amazing gifts. One little girl even got a Barbie Dream House, which was something I had always wanted through-out my childhood. I excitedly unwrapped my present and saw that my gift was just a plastic toy makeup set, the kind of thing you would get at the dollar store. My sister got a coloring book.

Although ordinarily I would have been overjoyed to get an unexpected toy, I felt horrible that night because I had compared my toy to the toys of the other children. The myth I had been taught was that Santa gave good toys to good children and bad toys to bad children, so did that mean that the other children at the event were better than me? At the time, that was the conclusion I had made. I couldn't have been older than 5 years old and I had already determined that I wasn't as good as other kids.

There's a quote by Theodore Roosevelt that states "comparison is the thief of joy". There was nothing wrong with the toy I received. There was nothing wrong with my parents having got me that toy over something grander. Honestly, that was the appropriate type of gift for an event like that. What made it "bad" was that I assigned it a negative value by comparing it to the gifts other children received at the event.

In comparison to the other toys, mine was probably one of the ones with the least value. I remember it being the least, but there were probably other sensible parents that went to the dollar store as well. My notion of what was "enough" was skewed that night by other people's concepts of "enough". Clearly, there were parents at that event who would have thought my gift wasn't enough for their child. Because of that, I decided that my gift wasn't enough and that I wasn't enough either.

Has your concept of what is "enough" been skewed by comparing yourself to others? This is something that I see a lot in my office. To better illustrate my point, let me tell you about my client Trina. Trina was going to school here on a student visa. Her family was extremely poor, the kind of poverty that we just don't see in the United States. It had taken an incredible amount of hardship just to pay for the plane ticket to fly here, but she did it. She got into a good University and graduated with honors.

Trina had a difficult time finding a job after graduating and she really needed to in order to get a work visa so she could stay in the country and move closer to citizenship. She finally found something. The pay was on the low end of what a graduate with her degree could expect and the agency didn't have a great reputation, but it was a job and it meant she could stay in the Country. Trina knew she should have been overjoyed, but she felt horrible about her situation instead.

When Trina compared herself to the other people in her graduating class, she found that they had been able to find a job much faster and the jobs were better paying and at better agencies. Based on this information, Trina then decided that her classmates must be better than her. Her achievement of beating the odds and moving closer towards citizenship now felt like a failure. Trina became very depressed.

One of the things that really helped Trina was to put things in perspective. Her classmates had opportunities, supports, and resources that she simply never had. She would have done just as well if not better if she had had those same advantages. Furthermore, she realized that although they had advantages over her now, there was nothing to say that Trina wouldn't be able to catch up to them later on in her career. Finally, a job hardly determines a person's self-worth.

Who is someone that you compare yourself to that when you do it makes you feel like you are not as good as they are? Now,

I want you to ask yourself, what are the core differences that make you different from this person? How have those differences contributed to that person achieving more than you have at this time? What could you do to level the playing field?

When we really take the time to examine someone we envy, we often find that they are really not that enviable; that they have flaws just like we do. Very often my clients will find that the person they envy doesn't have anything that they don't have, other than perhaps the will to take the things they want out of life. Often we find that their achievements are not better than ours, just different.

I remember that towards the beginning of my career, like Trina, I was not feeling great about what I had achieved. I was at the bottom of the totem pole and I didn't like it. I would look at other therapists and where they were in their career and would wish that I was there too. Then I realized that these were people that had twenty years' experience over me. Of course, they were in a different place in their career!

Once you really start examining other people objectively, you realize that no one's better than anyone else. Some people were born with more advantages, but that doesn't make them *better*, it makes them lucky! And just because they were born with more advantages doesn't mean that you aren't capable of catching up to them. So-called "birth rights" can only get you so far in life. At some point you have to start working really hard if you want to keep up the momentum. People whom were born with disadvantages know how to work really hard to get what they want. That may be an advantage that you have that the privileged doesn't.

Keeping the stakes low

People with low self-esteem know all about keeping the stakes low. When your self-esteem is painfully low, naturally you don't want to take any risks to make your self-esteem any lower. You worry that if you were to put all of your effort into something and then failed anyway that it would be such a blow to your self-esteem that you couldn't survive it. So, you keep the stakes low by dating people who really aren't good enough for you, by taking on jobs that are below your skill-set, and by never challenging yourself.

What a lot of people who take this strategy don't realize is that by doing so they are making their self-esteem even worse. It makes sense if you think about it: Someone who behaves this way does so because they believe that self-esteem is fueled by achievement and acceptance. But here's the thing, by never achieving anything and being "accepted" by people you find unacceptable, you just further feed into the notion that you are not good enough.

Keeping the stakes low in this manner does nothing for your self-esteem. It just keeps you in a perpetual state of wishing your life was different and feeling bad about yourself. Would it surprise you if I told you that people with high self-esteem kept the stakes low too? It's actually true. The difference is that they go about it in a very different way.

For people with high self-esteem the stakes are very low in life, as they should be. When they are in a relationship with someone, the stakes are low for them. They aren't worried about if the relationship doesn't work out because they know that they can just get a new relationship if it doesn't. Compare this to someone with low self-esteem whom the stakes are very high when they are in a relationship. To them, if the relationship doesn't work out, it means that they are unlovable, so they hold onto the relationship as if it were a matter of life and death. Those are very high stakes.

Would it surprise you if I told you that achievements were a result of high self-esteem and not the other way around? A lot of people think that high self-esteem comes from having achieved a lot, but it doesn't. Without self-esteem, the stakes are too high to take the risks necessary to achieve things in life. Everyone who has ever started a business or put themselves out there for a promotion knows that failure is a possibility. When you have low self-esteem, failure is not an option so most people will not even try. Or if they do try, they'll be so cautious about it as to not even have a real chance of succeeding. When you have high self-esteem, you know that if you fail you'll just try again or go a different path; it's not a big deal.

In this day and age, there are very few things where the stakes are truly high. There are very few decisions where once made, could not be unmade or mended. As a therapist, I often encounter people who come to me and tell me that their life has been completely ruined. Very rarely is that actually the case. In most cases people are able to pick themselves up and are actually better off in the end because of the "tragedy" that occurred.

What is something you want to do but haven't because the stakes have seemed too high? I want you to think through what would happen if you had tried and failed. Imagine what you would do immediately after you failed. Would you be alright? What would your life be like one year after the failure? What would it be like five years later? Most people find that in the grand scheme of things that they would be alright if they failed. In that case, the stakes are low indeed.

Many people tell me that they know that the stakes are low, but to their toxic family, they are quite high. They know that if they failed their family would lord it over them and make them feel horrible about it. This is why I instructed you earlier in the book to stop telling your family both about your successes and failures. This is hard to do at first, but once you start to experience the emotional freedom that comes from it, it becomes very easy to keep doing it.

Conclusion

The important thing I want you to take away from this is that you are enough. Other people are not better than you. They may have been born with some advantages that you were not, but that does not make them better than you. You are enough, simply for being you. There is nothing you need to do to increase your self-esteem other than to realize that, and once you have your self-esteem, it is not something that anyone can ever take away from you.

Entire books have been written on how to increase your self-esteem, and certainly reading this one chapter won't be enough for everyone. There are no overnight miracles when it comes to low self-esteem. If low self-esteem is something that you've been really struggling with, then perhaps the best thing you can do is to see a therapist.

The causes and contributors to low self-esteem can be quite unique and vary from person to person. That is why it can be difficult to get the solution you are looking for from a self-help book when it comes to this topic. When someone writes a book on self-esteem, they can only provide general guidelines that they hope will be helpful to most people. When you see a therapist, the therapist creates a strategy that is tailor made just for you. This is just one of the advantages of seeing a therapist.

12

Finding your life path

Cassidy was a less-than-Junior executive. Still, she was just happy to have gotten a job at a Fortune 500 company in the big city. Nothing ever seemed to come easy for her, but she found that so long as she kept persisting she would eventually reach her goals. She had been lucky enough to marry a great man and now was trying to get her career to be as great as her marriage.

There was talk at work about Cassidy possibly getting a promotion. It wasn't a sure thing yet, but Cassidy didn't want to do anything to jeopardize her promotion. The promotion would involve Cassidy traveling to the company's various offices and whipping them into shape. This could be the big break she's been hoping for. There's only one problem: Cassidy has always had a fear of driving and this new position would involve lots of it.

Cassidy always had a lot of anxiety about driving. She didn't get her driver's license until she was in her 20's, which was something she felt very embarrassed about. Even after she got her license, she drove very little and after moving to the city she drove even less, preferring to take the bus or subway. Eventually she sold her car and used the money to pay off her credit card debt. She hadn't driven in years.

She really wanted this promotion and was worried that her fear of driving would keep her from being able to succeed in her new position. She had thought about seeing a therapist off and on for probably her whole life. It was always for reasons other than her driving phobia, but for some reason she had never gone. In the end she had always handled these difficulties on her own. However, when it came to issues involving her career, Cassidy had no problem doing whatever it took, even if it meant seeing a therapist.

At her first appointment with the therapist, Cassidy found therapy to be a much different experience than she would have thought. She had assumed that seeing a therapist would be a lot like seeing any other kind of medical provider: cold, introspective, and all business. Instead she found her therapist to be warm, chatty, and very personable. This made Cassidy feel much more comfortable and at ease talking to the therapist. She found that talking to a therapist didn't feel that much different from talking to a best friend.

As therapy progressed, Cassidy found that she could be more open with her therapist than she could even be with herself. Just by talking to the therapist, she was realizing things about herself that she had never realized before. One of the things that she realized that really surprised her was that her fear of driving had nothing to do with being afraid of dying in a car accident.

Cassidy had spent much of her teenage years feeling suicidal, so the thought of death didn't really scare her. She also imagined that when someone dies in a car accident that the death is very sudden, so you basically die before you even realize what has happened. To Cassidy, there was nothing really scary about that. She also didn't think it was likely that she would die in a car accident. The thought of getting into a car accident didn't scare her either. All you do is pay the $500 deductible and you get a new car. It was an inconvenience but hardly anything to be scared about.

So if risking her life or crashing the car doesn't scare her, then why did she experience such panic while driving? Cassidy was especially anxious when driving in the winter, making U-Turns on busy streets, and parallel parking. Not out of fear of getting into an accident, but for some other reason. What was it?

Cassidy's therapist helped Cassidy realize that what was really causing her fear of driving was performance anxiety. Deep down, she had a fear of being harshly judged for the way she drove. She was afraid of being embarrassed or ridiculed while trying to parallel park, take U-turns, etc. Deep down, more than anything,

Cassidy was afraid of being made-fun-of and shamed; of being "inadequate".

When Cassidy's therapist said she wanted to learn more about Cassidy's childhood, Cassidy thought that it was because the therapist was trying to milk her for more sessions. "I don't see the relevance of talking about my childhood", Cassidy said. "All of that stuff has been resolved. I haven't had any contact with my family in years. I've moved past it." But Cassidy's therapist persisted and eventually Cassidy gave in and started to talk about it.

While talking about her childhood, something happened that Cassidy didn't expect: tears flowed out of her eyes non-stop. She couldn't stop crying. She turned into a blubbering, sobbing mess. Still, her therapist encouraged her to keep talking about it and to get it out. Cassidy had no idea just how much pain she had been holding in. Prior to that therapy session, she hadn't cried in years.

Cassidy revealed that in her family, she was the "comic relief". Her siblings would constantly make fun of her. Whenever she tried to make a serious suggestion, her family would just say "Oh Cassidy" and everyone would laugh. Every little thing she did was the object of ridicule. It wasn't easy feeling like you were a joke.

In addition to never being taken seriously, Cassidy was also harshly criticized by her mother. Her mother would grab an inch of fat on her stomach and scold her. Her mother frequently made her go to bed hungry because she wasn't "as thin as she should be". Her appearance was constantly scrutinized and nit-picked.

Even Cassidy's intelligence was criticized. Cassidy got very bad performance anxiety when it came to doing tests and this would bring down her grades in school. Her teachers knew she was intelligent, yet her grades were sub-par. This led to her mother filing paperwork to have Cassidy legally deemed as having mental retardation. Cassidy was 14 when she was tested for mental retardation. At that point she had been ridiculed so much that she was starting to believe that perhaps she truly deserved that diagnosis. When Cassidy was found to have normal intelligence, her mother was furious and accused Cassidy of cheating the test in order to make her mother look bad. In the meantime, Cassidy's mother told anyone who would listen that her "daughter was retarded" and oh what a burden it was for her.

This experience did not cause Cassidy to give up academically. It actually just motivated her to try harder and Cassidy credits it for allowing her to have gotten as far as she has. It was a few years later that she learned that her mother just made up the whole thing about her having mental retardation so that she could collect social security money on Cassidy's behalf. Cassidy was furious. How could her mother do something like that? If her mother had managed to convince everyone that Cassidy had mental retardation that would have greatly limited what she could have done with her life. How incredibly selfish and cruel! This was when Cassidy starting pulling away from her family.

Her therapist helped Cassidy to understand that her fear of driving really didn't have much to do with driving at all. Cassidy was a fairly good driver. She had passed her driving test fine and had never even gotten a ticket or been in an accident. Driving was not the problem. The real problem was that deep down she believed that she was inadequate and inherently worthy of other people's ridicule. Despite the phony persona she had adopted of being a confident business woman, she was very insecure and this was the legacy of her dysfunctional family.

Suddenly, it all made sense to Cassidy: Her fear of driving, her insecurity about her appearance, why she always had to try so much harder in order to get ahead at work. It was all because of what her family had put her through. She thought that by freeing herself of them that she had moved past it all, but really that was just the beginning. Although her life had greatly improved since ending contact with them, she still had a long way to go.

Her therapist asked her where she thought she would be right now if she had been raised in a normal family. It wasn't something Cassidy had ever thought about before, but once she started thinking about it, she realized that she probably would not have been a business executive. She had only chosen this profession because she thought it was prestigious and was a way to "prove herself" to all the people that had made fun of her.

Art was something that had always interested Cassidy, but her artwork had always been discouraged by her mother. Her therapist encouraged Cassidy to start making art work again and to bring something she had made into her next appointment. It had been so long since Cassidy had created art that she honestly didn't know where to start. Not able to come up with any ideas, she decided to just make a more artistic version of her Company's logo.

When she showed her therapist what she had created, her therapist was very impressed. Cassidy wasn't sure how to take praise like this; it was certainly a new experience for her. Her therapist encouraged her to hang up the drawing in her cubicle at work for "inspiration". Cassidy reluctantly agreed. She really only hung it up because her therapist had suggested it, otherwise she would have never dared to do something like that.

When Cassidy's boss came over to her cubicle to talk to her more about the possible promotion, he noticed her drawing. He was also impressed with it. They talked about the promotion. He had decided that she wasn't quite right for the position; however, they did have an opening in their design department. Cassidy's face lit up at the suggestion. Seeing how pleased she was, he said he would definitely see what he could do to get her transferred.

It wasn't the "big break" Cassidy had been looking for previous to starting therapy; however working with art and design at a great company was certainly a dream come true for her authentic self; the self that Cassidy discovered was still there buried underneath all of her childhood traumas. Through therapy she was learning to let go of all of her anxieties, insecurities, and to start living a life more true to herself. Oh, and driving was no longer a problem either.

You've probably heard the saying "Life's a bitch and then you die". As a therapist, I've encountered many people who live and breathe by this philosophy. "You're telling me that I have a special purpose in life, but life's a bitch, Marina. Life is all about suffering, there's no way around it. It's like that for everyone." I disagree. I believe that life is meant to be enjoyed and I'll you why.

I'm going to make a spiritual argument and then I'll make a non-spiritual argument for why life is meant to be enjoyed. First, why would God create us? It's surprisingly not something that's ever addressed in the Bible. Many religions believe that we are created to be servants to God (this coincides with the "life is suffering" philosophy), but if God is all-powerful, why would he need servants? Why would he need us to worship and toil for him? That philosophy never made sense to me, although I understand that it makes sense to a lot of other people and that's okay.

I believe that the only reason why an omnipotent being would create us is out of love. God created the Universe and saw that it was good and wanted to share that joy with others, so he created us. He created us so we could enjoy his creation. God created us so we could enjoy life.

Even if you don't believe in God, which is also completely okay, the philosophy still makes sense. Life is still precious and time-limited. We still only have one life to live. Since we are only given one life and only a few decades of health in which to enjoy it; doesn't it make sense to enjoy it as much as possible? Doesn't it make sense to make the most of it in any way you can? Even if you believe in reincarnation, this is still the only time you will be able to live this particular life, so why not enjoy it?

Some of you reading this may be thinking right now "Believe me Marina; I would enjoy my life if I could, but I just can't make it happen. That's why I'm reading this book." Of course everyone wants to be happy and enjoy life, but not everyone is able to do that. I believe that one of the reasons for chronic unhappiness comes from being on the wrong life path. Once you get on the right path and start living a more authentic life, suddenly chronic unhappiness is no longer a problem anymore.

What is a life path?

When you were born, you were born with a special purpose in life. You were born with a unique gift that makes the world a better place. However, when you were born, your parents had other plans for you. They didn't like the idea of you finding your own path in life, and sought to steer you in a different direction; onto a path that was more pleasing to them but miserable for you.

This "steering" or "influencing" is not always done maliciously. There are a lot of people out there who just assume that everyone wants the same things in life or that the lessons they've learned in life are the same lessons you need to learn. Other people view their children as a type of property, where your destiny is theirs to choose. They believe that as a parent it's their job or right to steer your life in the direction they would like for it to go. However, we all have our own unique path to walk in life. I call this your life path.

Your life path is your purpose in life. When you are on your life path, you are able to enjoy life. You feel that your life has meaning and purpose. For instance, my life path is to provide guidance and nurturance to others. When I first started on the path, I provided guidance and nurturance for friends and even strangers. As the path progressed, I became a therapist. Then I started writing books that provided nurturance and guidance. As I continue to walk this path, it may lead to me doing other things, but I will still be providing nurturance and guidance to others in some capacity.

There have been many times when I took a wrong turn and was taken off the path. A couple years ago I got a job offer that would nearly double my income and I was seriously pursuing it. At first it seemed great, but as I got closer to sealing the deal, I started to feel depressed. I felt lethargic and listless. I realized that although the money would be great, it would be taking me off my life path. I decided I wanted to stay on my life path more than I wanted the money, since it was my life path that would ultimately lead to happiness in life, not money.

I've had many moments like that throughout the years where great opportunities came my way and at first I was excited about them, but once I realized that it meant taking me away from doing what I love, helping other people, I just couldn't do it. A rule I have for myself now is I don't take a job, no matter how great it is, if the thought of it doesn't put a smile on my face.   Doing counseling, providing guidance with my books, that's what makes me happy and so I continue on this path.

As you can see, your life path has a lot to do with the career you choose, but it also has to do with everything else too. It has to do with the friends you have and the company you keep. I do not spend time with people whom disrespect me or make me feel unwelcome. I also do not spend time with people whom for what-ever reason make me feel bad about myself or do not bring out the best in me. Part of this has to do with boundaries, but part of it also has to do with my life path. People who make me feel bad are not people who are on the same path as me. I feel happier and more fulfilled when I am spending time with people who are on the same path in life. You will know who those people are because they support you and bring out the best in you.

Aside from your job and the people you keep around you, your life path also has to do with how you spend your free time. I genuinely love psychology, so in my spare time I read research, write blog posts, and read books on psychology. I also try to help people as much as possible and as much as healthy boundaries will allow. To me, it really isn't "work". I just enjoy it and am lucky enough to be paid for it.

Hopefully you are starting to see how if one stays faithful to their life path that they can begin to craft a life that is true to oneself and enjoyable. Cassidy found that her life path was to create art and design that touched other people's souls and provided interest and enjoyment. She loved creating art and challenging herself creatively. For her, a life of art meant a life of fun and enjoyment. You can also have a life you love. The first step is finding your life path.

Finding your life path

Some of you may already know what your life path is; you just never had the courage to follow it until now. Others may find that they would love to be on their life path, they just don't know what it is. If you are having a hard time finding your life path, there are some mental exercises you can do to reveal what it is.

I used to buy a lottery ticket once per week. I wasn't very serious about it; it was just something I did because an old boyfriend convinced me it was a good thing to do. He would buy one once per week and he reasoned with me that it only cost a dollar but it had the potential to net you hundreds of millions of dollars in return, so I decided I would start doing it too. Then one day I really started to think about what it would mean if I actually won the lottery.

At first it seemed great. I would never have to worry about money again. I could buy a dream home or simply not have a permanent address and just travel around for the rest of my life. Then as I thought about it further I realized that it meant I wouldn't be a counselor anymore, or at least it would seriously limit my ability to be a counselor. I couldn't go back to an "ordinary life" after winning that much money and that meant no longer being a counselor as I knew it. I decided I would rather be a counselor and stopped buying lottery tickets.

To some people, my decision sounds crazy. They hear that and they think "Who wouldn't want to never work again?" But actually we know that many lottery winners do go back to work. After the initial thrills of winning the lottery wears off, people decide that they were happier working.

My question to you is: What would you do for work after you won the lottery? Sure, you would probably take off a couple of years to travel and whatnot, but what would you do afterwards? Taking time off to go back to school nor the money needed to start a business would be an issue after you won the lottery. You could do anything. So, what would it be?

I've always believed that the litmus test for if you are in the right job would be "What do you love doing so much that you would do it for free?" I find that many of my clients are already doing something they love for free, they just haven't figured out yet how to turn it into a job or career. Once you can figure out how to make a living doing something you love, you are on your life path.

Some people find that they have something that they love doing but that the service itself is not profitable and they then want their family to support them financially so they can pursue their dream. I think that an important thing about pursuing your dream is to also take responsibility for your dream. There are some dreams that will never be profitable and if that is the case then you either need to find a way to make it more profitable or live within your means.

I had a dream of being in private practice, but I knew it took two to three years to build a big enough case load before my business would be profitable. Although I believed in my dream, I also believed that it was not right to burden my dream onto others. What I ended up doing was I kept my fulltime job while I worked on building my private practice. There is a surprising amount of work that goes into "setting up" a business, and it took me a year of doing this before I got my first client. I only took clients at night and on weekends so I could continue working my day job. There was another year of working full time before I was able to start phasing out of my job so I could devote more time to building my private practice. During this time, I decreased my expenses to just the bare minimum so that if something unexpected happened to my private practice I wouldn't be financially destitute. It took another year until I was doing my private practice full time.

A lot of self-help books tell you that if you have a dream then you need to jump in full force, but as you can see, I didn't do that. I kept my day job for three years while building my business at the same time. I didn't jump in, I eased in. I still was able to achieve my dream, but I didn't infringe on anyone else's dream in the process and I think that's important.

A lot of people complain that "living your dream" and "following your life path" just isn't practical, but I beg to differ. I, as well as many of the people I know and have had as clients, are living our dreams and are doing so in a way that is practical. I was able to remain practical by easing into my private practice. I took the time to consult with my husband and tweaked my business plan as many times as necessary in order to keep it practical and feasible. You can do the same thing.

Remember, the whole point of being on your life path is to enjoy your life. I knew I wouldn't be able to enjoy my life if I spent the first three years of my private practice stressed out about how I was going to pay my bills. If you find "living your dream" to be stressful and a hardship, then you aren't doing it right. You need to take a step back and find a way to make it more realistic and practical to you.

Another question you need to think about is: What do you think you would be doing with your life right now if you had been raised in a family that wasn't toxic? Really take some time to think about this one. Most of my clients find that there are a lot of difficulties in their life that can be traced back to the dysfunctional manner in which they were raised. It doesn't mean that your life would have been perfect, but you may be surprised what is and isn't attributed to your childhood.

Cassidy was surprised to find that her driving phobia was connected to her childhood performance anxiety and the near-constant criticism and ridicule she received from her family. She was also surprised to find that once she had resolved those issues that she no longer wanted the promotion at work. She realized that her true passion was for art and design and if she had been raised in a normal family she probably would have been an artist all along. Art was what gave her life meaning and purpose and was what she truly enjoyed.

What brings you joy? Your life path is very much tied to doing the things you love. Though I think it's important to remind people that we all have multiple things we enjoy doing, but some things are hobbies while other things are careers. For instance, I love swimming, hiking, traveling, playing with my cats, doing crafts, etc, but I wouldn't be happy with any of those things being turned ininto a career. However, my career is also something that I love and it allows me to do the other things that I love as hobbies.

When do you feel the most adequate and accomplished? This question may help you separate the hobbies from a future career. Hobbies don't make me feel adequate or accomplished, they're just fun and I do them for that reason and nothing more. However, I feel the most adequate and accomplished after I have really helped someone. What are things you can do that make you feel this way and give you a feeling of pride?

One of my clients felt really torn about her life path. She had worked in marketing, specifically in writing copy, and felt torn about it. She was really good at her what she did, but believed that she wasn't "making a difference" with her life. She had decided that marketing was basically consumerism and the devil's work. She didn't see how she was helping people.

I was able to help her see that she was helping people. As a small business owner, my dream could have never been realized without marketing. Likewise, people who really needed a product or service would never know about it if not for marketing. She was helping people; she just never realized it before. So when trying to determine your life path, don't get too hung up on whether your "making a difference" or not. If you have a passion for it and act with authenticity and positive intention, then you are doing good with your life.

You may also find that discovering your life path is a process of trial and error. It certainly was that way for me. It's really just a matter of experimenting until you find a life that works for you. It may seem like a lot of work at first, but in the end you get to live a life you love and I think that's well worth the effort.

It's also important to realize that your life can change and you can still remain on the same path even though things are changing. My life and career have changed a lot over the past decade, but I have remained on the same path. Although I set goals and try to plan for my future, the truth is I don't really know where my path will lead me. I know that wherever it goes it will be a good thing, and that leaves me feeling both secure and excited for the future ahead.

Conclusion

Everything in this book has been leading up to this moment, where you find your life path. First, you learned about your toxic family and came to understand that you were not the cause of their dysfunction. Then you learned to set firm boundaries with both them and the other people in your life. You took yourself out of the equation and changed the rules. You stopped playing the game and started surrounding yourself with more positive people. You started having relationships that were mutually beneficial and not based on exploitation. You realized you were enough and now have set foot on your life path.

Does this mean the journey's over? For some people reading this book, the journey has just begun. Perhaps by reading this book you have taken the first step towards a happier and more authentic life. For others, reading this book was just one of many steps towards sustained wellness. We're all at different stages in our journey; the important thing is that we just keep moving.

I put a lot of love into this book. I really do hope that you enjoyed it and got a lot out of it, but I know how difficult it is trying to recover from a toxic family. If you've finished reading this book and still feel like you haven't found all the answers, than I really do urge you to consider seeing a therapist. It doesn't mean that you're a failure; it just means that you need a more custom approach than a book can provide.

References

Allen, D. M. (2010). *How Dysfunctional Families Spur Mental Disorders: A balanced approach to resolve problems and reconcile relationships*. Santa Barbara, CA: Praeger.

Amato, P. R. (2010). Research on divorce: Continuing trends and new developments. *Journal of Marriage and Family, 72*(3), 650-666.

Bader, Shannon M.; Welsh, Robert; Scalora, Mario J. (2010). Recidivism among female child molesters. *Violence and Victims, 25* (3): 349–62.

Becker, J. and Murphy, W. (1998). What we know and don't know about assessing and treating sex offenders. *Psychology, Public Policy and Law* (4): 116-137.

Burns, D. (1999). *Ten days to self-esteem* (Reprint ed.). New York: William Morrow Paperbacks.

Button, D., Parker, L., Gealt, R. (2008). The effects of sibling violence on high risk behaviors. *American Society of Criminology.*

Campbell, W. K., Foster, C. A., & Finkel, E. J. (2002). Does self-love lead to love for others?: A story of narcissistic game playing. *Journal of personality and social psychology, 83*(2), 340.

David, A. S. (2005). Psychosis following head injury: a critical review. *Journal of Neurology, Neurosurgery & Psychiatry*, i53-i60.

DeOllos, I. Y., & Kapinus, C. A. (2002). Aging childless individuals and couples: Suggestions for new directions in research. *Sociological Inquiry, 72*(1), 72-80.

Dweck, C. S. (2007). Can personality be changed? The role of beliefs in personality and change. *Current Directions in Psychological Science,* 391-394.

Eitle, D. (2010). General strain theory, persistence, and desistance among young adult males. *Journal of criminal justice, 38*(6), 1113-1121.

Herpertz, S. C., & Sass, H. (2000). Emotional deficiency and psychopathy. *Behavioral Sciences & the Law, 18*(5), 567-580.

Iribarren, J. (2005). Post-traumatic stress disorder: Evidence-based research for the third millennium. *Evidence-based Complementary and Alternative Medicine,* 503-512.

Lou, Y. L. L., Cai, H., Song, H. (2014). A behavioral genetic study of intrapersonal and interpersonal dimensions of narcissism. *PLoS ONE,* e93403.

Mcallister, T. W. (2010). Psychiatric disorders and traumatic brain injury: What is the connection?. *Psychiatric Annals,* 533-539.

Rosenberg, R. (2013). *The human magnet syndrome: Why we love people who hurt us.* : PESI Publishing & Media.

Samenow, S. (2012). *Inside the criminal mind:* Revised and updated edition. Random House LLC.

Stout, M. (2005). *The sociopath next door: The ruthless versus the rest of us.* New York: Broadway Books.

Umberson, D., Pudrovska, T., & Reczek, C. (2010). Parenthood, childlessness, and well-being: A life course perspective. *Journal of Marriage and Family, 72* (3), 612-629.

U.S. Department of Health and Human Services, Administration for Children and Families, Administration on Children, Youth and Families, Children's Bureau. (2013). *Child Maltreatment 2012.*

White, L. K., Booth, A., & Edwards, J. N. (1986). Children and marital happiness: Why the negative correlation?. *Journal of Family Issues, 7*(2), 131-147.

Wikstrom, P. (2004). *Individual risk, life-style risk and adolescent offending.*

About the Author

Marina Williams, MA, LMHC is a Licensed Mental Health Counsellor who specializes in treating relationship issues, depression, and anxiety disorders. She graduated with a Masters Degree in Clinical Psychology from Bridgewater State University. She currently works in private practice, offering both individual and couples counselling in the Hyde Park neighbourhood of Boston, Massachusetts.

In addition to providing counselling, Marina Williams works as an independent author. She has written and published the books "Taking Yourself Out of the Equation: And Taking Your Life Back From Your Dysfunctional Family", "Couples Counselling: A Step by Step guide for Therapists", "Tricks of the Trade: How to be a Top Notch Mental Health Counsellor in an Age of Competition", "Results Directed Therapy: An Integrative and Dynamic Approach to Psychotherapy", and "Ending the Power Struggle: A Step by Step Guide for Couples Counsellors".

Marina Williams also has a number of resources available for therapists who are looking for support or further training. She is the founder and creator of TherapistCE.com, an affordable continuing education provider for therapists. She also has a blog intended for other therapists that can be found on her website MarinaWilliamsLMHC.com. The website for her private practice is CounselingWithMarina.com.

26128824R00147

Printed in Great Britain
by Amazon